Contents

Jo Roll

Occasional Paper
number 13

What is a Family?

benefit models and social realities

Family Policy Studies Centre

This occasional paper, like all those in the series, represents the views of the authors and not necessarily those of the Family Policy Studies Centre.

The author Jo Roll is a Senior Research Officer at the Family Policy Studies Centre

Acknowledgements The author would like to thank all those who provided valuable advice for this project funded by the Joseph Rowntree Foundation. They include the participants in the advisory seminar held at the instigation of the Joseph Rowntree Foundation, as well as a number of others who were kind enough to spare the time to comment on an earlier draft.

Special thanks are due to Meredith Ann Edwards for her book, 'The Income Unit in the Australian Tax and Social Security Systems', published by the Institute for Family Studies, Melbourne, Australia, 1984, which provided much inspiration for this project.

published by
Family Policy Studies Centre
231 Baker Street
London NW1 6XE

ISBN 0 907051-59-6

Design and print by Intertype

Does it matter what a family is?

What is a family? There are many different ways of answering the question and these might involve genetic ties, legal ties or simply the nature of the relationship. It is possible to argue at length about which is the right answer but, meanwhile, government laws and institutions have drawn up their own definitions which have a real impact on people's lives.

Among the official definitions, the 'benefit' family is one which has a particularly marked effect because it can result in more money for some and no money for others. Living with a partner, for example, can deprive you of benefit, entitle you to a larger amount, or make no difference at all, depending on the situation and the rules for different benefits.

The fact that government policies have their own explicit and implicit assumptions about the family is not the only reason why the definition matters. 'The family' itself has been changing rapidly; and this has led to the question whether official definitions are realistic or left over from previous eras when circumstances and attitudes were different.

Current definitions have come under attack from several quarters, representing diverse attitudes about the way that people *should* live as well as diverse responses to the ways in which they *do* live.

There are, for example, those who feel that 'traditional' values need to be upheld and that state benefits undermine the 'traditional' family; there is the feminist critique of women's financial dependence on men and the elements within the benefit system that reinforce it; and there is the libertarian emphasis on personal autonomy and the rights of individuals within whatever family or grouping they choose to associate themselves.

Proposals for reform point in contradictory directions, sometimes even when they stem from the same 'camp'. On the one hand, some would widen official definitions of the family to include relationships which are not currently taken into account. On the other, some would narrow them to the point where the individual becomes the basic unit; not forgetting those who would strengthen existing definitions.

Policies have responded to some extent. Income tax, for example, has been reformed so that husbands and wives are now to a large extent taxed separately as individuals instead of as a single unit. Indeed, almost every area of family law has been under scrutiny in recent years, even if reforms have not always resulted.

As far as benefits are concerned, the Beveridge Plan, out of which the present system has developed, treated married couples, not just as a single unit, but as one in which men were the breadwinners and women the housewives and childrearers. Husbands were expected to earn and receive benefit on behalf of the couple while wives were expected to give up paid work and become financially dependent on their husbands.

Perhaps Beveridge's attitude is best encapsulated in the following quotation from the report:

'The attitude of the housewife to gainful employment outside the house is not and should not be the same as that of a single woman. She has other duties.'[1]

The benefit system has undoubtedly adapted since the 1940s when the report was published. For example, the rules now discriminate less between the sexes within a married couple and, in some circumstances, it is easier for married women to qualify independently. But the couple unit has not been abandoned nor has the assumed division of labour between a breadwinner and a dependant.

Have the reforms which have taken place gone far enough? This Paper aims to contribute to the debate on this issue in the following way:

Chapter 1 discusses the need for policies to adapt to the realities of life today and summarises the way that policies have responded to family change and diversity.

Chapter 2 concentrates on the benefit system, stressing the fact that there are several different definitions of the 'benefit' family in use today and that some of these apply to different aspects of the same benefit.

Chapter 3 examines trends and possible future directions in the way that the 'benefit' family is defined.

Chapter 4 discusses some issues which have arisen in the light of existing living and working arrangements.

Chapter 5 discusses the need for reform.

These chapters need to be supplemented with the Appendix, which describes present benefit rules in more detail and explains technical terms. As far as possible, it is up to date at April 1991.

Chapter 1

A realistic assessment of the situation?

Unforeseen consequences

If policies are out of touch with reality, they run the risk of failure. Prohibition in the United States during the 1920s and 30s, which has featured in many gangster films, is a well-known example of a policy which had to be abandoned because of its unforeseen and undesired consequences.

Unrealistic assumptions about the family can also lead to failure. This point is often made about several of the pre-Beveridge attempts to reduce public expenditure on benefits by relying on family obligations instead. It has been argued that these policies were not as successful as their advocates hoped because the version of family responsibilities which they tried to impose was widely regarded as unreasonable.[2]

The 'liable relative' rules, which can be traced back to the 1601 Poor Law, are often quoted in this context. They required husbands to maintain wives and grandparents to maintain grandchildren but not vice versa. Parents and children were liable to maintain each other, although married daughters were exempt. The rules were adapted over time so that by the 1940s, various others, such as stepfathers and an 'illegitimate' child were added to the list.[3]

There is evidence that at times when these rules, or their application, were tightened up, they had unintended and unwanted consequences, not least of which was large scale avoidance. At the turn of the last Century, for example, some people 'lost touch' with their elderly parents in order to avoid paying maintenance for them.[4]

Similarly, the household means-test of the 1930s is widely aknowledged to have led to 'collusive desertion' and to the break up of families as younger members left. At one stage, in order to overcome the avoidance problem, the authorities were even driven to develop the notion of a 'constructive household', which included people no longer living there.[5]

The reforms of 1948 drastically cut back the range of liable relatives and the household means test was abolished. But it is interesting to note the views embodied in the changes. In particular, it was regarded as unreasonable that fathers should be dependent on adult sons whereas a wife's dependence on her husband was regarded as normal[6] and spouse's liability for each other remains in the rules today (see Chapter 2).

But it is not only government policies which are likely to be affected by family change. A much more recent example is provided by the Abbey National's experience in 1989 when it decided to issue free shares to its former members as it shed its building society status and became a public limited company.

The trouble arose because many couples had joint accounts or joint mortgages and so, under building society law, were treated as one. It had long been the rule that the first named person was the member and, in practice, most couples tend to put the man's name first, that is, Mr. and Mrs. rather than Mrs. and Mr. The result was that it was usually the man who received the free shares and there were some very angry protests from the women.

The changeover from building society to plc was a time of upheaval and it generated a considerable volume of mail to headquarters about numerous aspects of the change. But of all these, 40% came from women and about half of the women's letters were about the joint membership system. Typical protests were:

'The scheme is unfair, my husband and I should get half the shares each', or even, 'My husband and I should get a full set of shares each', or 'I should get the shares — I opened the account, then added his name later', and 'We have two accounts. One is for me, one for my husband. We only put his name first as that is the expected way you do it', and 'I pay the mortgage (we've split up) but his name is still on the account as first named.'[7]

In practice, as the Abbey National pointed out, some of these issues could be resolved by claims against the husband under family law, although the procedures might have been rather laborious. However, the incident does appear to show how problems can arise when couples are treated as a single unit and when men, even if inadvertently, are given preferential treatment.

The model family

nucleer
but married

At the heart of many current discussions about the family lies a model with which present ways of life are contrasted. This consists of a married couple living together with their dependent child(ren). It is often envisaged in a 'nuclear' household, that is, separate from other relatives, with the man as breadwinner and the woman as housewife and childrearer. But it is the institution of marriage which is central to the model.

Insofar as it is based on legal status, this model has the advantage that it is relatively easy to use in order to characterise real life situations. In general, a couple is either married or not married as far as the law is concerned, whatever else may be happening in practice.

However, once it is accepted that the married family may not be the only kind of family, it becomes much harder to say what a family is. This is partly because living arrangements in practice are much harder to categorise, as the difficulties in defining cohabitation for social security purposes illustrate all too clearly (see Chapter 4).

But it is also a question of deciding what is (or are) the essential element(s) of a family. Is it responsibility for a child, for example? If so, does anyone bringing up a child become a family, regardless of their relationship to the child or to anyone else?

There may be no single answer. Different definitions may be necessary for different purposes and, for some people, the answer also involves a value judgment about the relationships which are to be approved and those which are to be condemned as undesirable.

Here, family change and diversity is used simply as shorthand to describe living and working arrangements which depart from the model. The intention is not to imply any value judgment about any of them, although some may take this as a value judgment in itself.

Changes over time have undoubtedly taken place and these suggest that, although the model type of family is by no means extinct, other living arrangements have become far more common than they were at the time the present benefit system was being set up. But this is not necessarily to say that the model was ever wholly realistic or that people believe that it was. At least some of the apparent increase in diversity may simply reflect the fact that people are more aware of it.

It is an open question whether this diversity is temporary while society moves towards a new, relatively uniform set of arrangements or whether it will be a permanent, and possibly multiplying, development. Is marriage to be replaced by something else, for example? Or change its nature? Or survive as only one among several ways of establishing a long-term relationship?

Family change and diversity

What are the changes which have taken place? Soaring divorce and tumbling marriage rates, more old people and violent swings in the number of school leavers, more than a quarter of babies born outside marriage, either to women on their own or to 'cohabiting' couples: these are just some of the moving pieces in the kaleidscope which family and living patterns have recently become.[8]

The result is that, in contrast to the model family described above, only half of babies can now expect to spend all of their childhood with both their natural married parents[9] and the types of family (step, lone parent, cohabiting parent etc.) which they may live in, or pass through, are many and varied.

The vast increase in the employment of married women is another of the well-known changes and, in contrast to the assumption made by Beveridge (see Chapter 2), it is not usually marriage itself which makes a difference to women's employment patterns but the birth of a baby.[10]

However, in spite of the increase, women's employment patterns still do not resemble men's. Most mothers take several years off, many return to lower level jobs at lower rates of pay, and most of them work part time.[11] Even if women do not have children, they are more likely to have a break in their employment for other reasons, such as caring for an adult.[12]

Regional and cultural differences also contribute to the diversity of family life. For example, women's employment varies between regions because of the type of local industry[13] and extended families living in one household are more common among people of Indian, Pakistani and Bangladeshi origin.[14]

High levels of unemployment in the 1980s have disproportionately struck certain regions, age groups and ethnic minorites. They have also increased the possibility of family unemployment. Both members of a couple may be unemployed, as well as young people still living in the parental home and other members of the wider family.

Financial arrangements within families also vary. The ideal of 'sharing' is widely held but only 1 in 5 couples say that their resources are genuinely pooled in practice;[15] and numerous surveys have found that it is women who generally carry out the bulk of household tasks, even when both partners are employed, although women who are employed full-time do seem to do less housework than other women in couples.[16]

Married couples rarely keep their finances totally separate and doing so has been described as a 'Yuppie' way of life[17] because it is more common among the younger ones with higher incomes. Cohabiting couples are also more inclined to manage their finances independently.[18] But as they also tend to be younger, it is not certain whether they will share more when and if they marry or whether they are part of a culture which values independence in financial matters.

After 1992, when internal borders between member states of the European Community are due to be abolished, further change is likely. Long-distance commuting from poorer to richer regions within Britain already takes place[19] and has opened up the possibility that families may be split for most of the week, while families split between countries are already a feature of life for immigrants to this country.

Attitudes to family life and the issues on which attention is focused have changed as well. The past and projected rise in the numbers of people over pension age, for example, has focused attention on relations between adult children and their parents and stimulated discussion about the role of the 'extended family'.

At the other end of the adult age range, there is the question of who is going to be responsible for young people if their entry into the labour market and opportunity to earn an independent living is to be delayed a few years while they are educated and trained.

But just as living and working arrangements are diverse, so are attitudes and values. Given the extent to which the benefit system is based on assumptions about employment (see Chapter 2), the change in attitudes to women's employment is perhaps one of the most striking. These also illustrate the danger of overestimating the impact of a particular trend.

In 1987, less than half (45%) of working age women said that a married woman with a child under school age 'ought to' stay home — a large fall compared with 1965, when over three quarters (78%) said so. But when a general sample of adults was asked the same question, over half (57%) said she 'ought to' stay home.

As for the opposite, that is, whether she 'ought to' work, hardly anyone said that she should. Even if all her children had left school, less than 1 in 10 thought that she 'ought to' work.[20] However, these answers need to be interpreted in the light of other options which respondents were given, as the table below shows.

		Ought to work	Up to her	Only if really needs money	Ought to stay at home
Single woman with:					
no family responsibilities	%	70	28	2	-
Married woman with:					
no children	%	23	70	6	-
children under school age	%	1	19	22	57
children at school	%	2	50	32	15
children but all left school	%	8	82	9	1

Source: British Social Attitudes Survey, the 1987 Report (p192), see reference 16.

Policies respond

These and other departures from the old model family have led to many policy changes. In recent years, most areas connected with the family justice system have been re-examined. But the winds of change have also reached further afield, including tax, social security and inheritance laws. As social security is the main subject of the rest of the Paper, this chapter outlines some background developments.

Mary Whitehouse's letter to the Times calling for policies to reverse the changes in family life[21] represents one pole of opinion in favour of the model family. Policy makers themselves have tended to be more wary of attempting such a task or of making statements that explicitly condemn new family forms, whatever their policies may actually do.

For example, although 'family stability' is one of the eleven objectives which the government has set out for social security,[22] the White Paper 'Children come First' declares that:

"The parents of a child may separate. In some instances the parents may not have lived together as a family at all… Government cannot ensure that families stay together. [23]

Where there has been a direct policy response, sometimes this has resulted in changed objectives and sometimes in changed methods designed to achieve the old objectives more effectively. The Budget speech of 1988 made by Nigel Lawson, illustrates both reactions. On the one hand:

'The present system of taxation of married couples goes back 100 years. It taxes the income of a married woman as if it belonged to her husband. Quite simply, that is no longer acceptable.' [24]

But, on the other hand, because the tax system behaved as if cohabiting couples did not exist, these couples sometimes did better than married ones and:

'It is clearly wrong that some couples should find themselves paying more tax simply because they are married. I propose to put that right.' [25]

As these examples also illustrate, for the individuals concerned, the recognition of their situation can be to their advantage or to their disadvantage. Married women gained from the tax changes but cohabiting couples lost.

Either way, as the next section will show, policies may respond by extending the family, by shrinking it, or leaving it as it is. They could bring a wider range of relationships into the family net, restrict the range (which, at the limit, means to the individual) or attempt to reinforce the institution of marriage on which the model family is based.

The extending family or the shrinking family? Perhaps the single most notable extension to the model family for policy purposes has been the recognition of heterosexual cohabitation, although this is relatively recent and a cohabiting couple is still not treated in exactly the same way as a married couple.

The Law Commission has described the 1976 Violence and Domestic Proceedings Act as 'entirely novel' in that it recognised the rights of cohabitees to protection from the violence of their partners. Cohabitees are also recognised in such areas as housing tenancies, compensation for criminal injuries and fatal accidents, and may also be covered under the wider category of 'dependant', as under the 1975 Inheritance Act, which allows dependants to make claims on the estate of a dead person.[26]

Other extensions were made by the 1989 Children Act,[27] for example. It gives children more say over decisions that affect them and incorporates the 1987 Family Law Reform Act which, with a few exceptions, equalises the status of children born inside and outside marriage. Unmarried fathers are also given more rights, although they do have to take formal steps in order to acquire 'parental responsibility', either by agreement with the mother or by means of a Court Order.

The Act also gives more rights to stepparents and other non-parents. For example, anyone with an interest in the child's welfare may be able to apply for Residence and Contact Orders, that is for the child to live with or visit them. However, some people, and that normally includes parents, will qualify to apply as of right while others will have to go through a two stage process by first getting the leave of the Court.

Another interesting feature of the Act is that, while it reinforces the obligations of natural parents by establishing a concept of 'parental responsibility' which it is very difficult to lose, it also creates the possibility that several people will have 'parental responsibility' as other people can acquire it.

Widening the net further, a recent report on conciliation concluded that children's ties with grandparents impinge so strongly on the nuclear family that they ought not to be ignored in family disputes. It also argued that grandparents themselves are adopting a higher profile by setting up groups to advise and assist in resolving access and custody difficulties. However, the extent to which they are actually involved is controversial.[28]

As for the shrinking family, the Immigration Act 1988 abolished the right of British and long-settled Commonwealth citizens to be joined by their wives and children. This is an example where shrinking the family reduced certain people's rights. But this is not a necessary consequence of such change. The Equal Pay and Sex Discrimination Acts of the 1970s, on the other hand, which have indirectly contributed to the independent treatment of husbands and wives, can be regarded as measures which have given women more rights.

Since April 1990 a wife's income no longer belongs to her husband for tax purposes, although marriage still entitles a couple to an extra allowance which is only available to the wife if the husband cannot use it up. The 'tax family' has narrowed in other ways too. During the 1980s, several small allowances — for a dependent relative, a housekeeper and the services of a daughter or son — were abolished. These followed in the wake of the child allowance which had been abolished in the 1970s.

The Poll Tax, introduced in England and Wales in 1990, was much heralded as a tax based on the individual and it certainly differed from the old rates which were based on the household. But it contained several contradictions and was, in fact, more of a hybrid. The individual aspect .was that everyone over the age of 18, with a very few exceptions, had to pay and, even if they were entitled to a rebate, they had to pay one fifth.

But as some people have no income, someone is going to have to pay for them. The Institute for Fiscal Studies has calculated, for example, that at least 16% of the electorate are married women who are not working, and, although this does not necessarily mean that they have no income, it suggests that there may be a sizeable group who cannot afford to pay.[29] The Poll Tax rules therefore ensure that couples are 'jointly and severally' liable for each other's bills.

The institution of marriage

It is apparent from this brief overview that the model family still survives in policy and legislation. Even among the examples mentioned, there have been limits to change. In particular, the institution of marriage has not been abandoned, although its nature may be questionned.

Indeed, following Nigel Lawson's Budget Statement quoted above, tax rules which happened to benefit cohabiting couples because they were treated as two separate people have recently been revised in order to bolster the institution of marriage.

Allowing the wife's income to be taxed independently can also be seen in this light as it effectively increased the allowances available to married people. However, most of the other changes worked by cutting the allowances available to the unmarried.

These included mortgage interest relief, which now relates to the property rather than to the individual (before cohabiting couples could get two lots of relief whereas married couples could only get one); the restriction of the additional allowance for a child to those without a cohabiting partner (before a cohabiting couple with two children were each able to claim the allowance for one child); and changes in the tax treatment of maintenance, which have generally reduced the amount of relief available.

The recognition of heterosexual cohabitees may not, in any case, be regarded as terribly revolutionary. It has been argued that, with few exceptions, laws have been worded so as to recognise relationships which are as marriage-like as possible. 'Mistresses', for example, that is those who have a regular relationship with a partner that they do not live with and who may be married to someone else have not generally been included.[30]

Finally, what about the institution of marriage itself, the essence of the model family? It is no longer an institution whose internal relations are entirely private and whose external relations are conducted by one person, the husband. But instead of developing into an equal partnership, which was one possibility, it has increasingly become an institution of two separate individuals whose individual rights are recognised.[31]

For example, separate property was established in 1882; with that came the capacity to draw up separate contracts, including a contract with the spouse; spouses may sue each other; domestic violence is now recognised and one partner may even be ordered from the home. To this list one could add the recent sentence for marital rape which made legal history by jailing a man even though the couple were not legally separated.[32]

As a consequence of these trends, one of the most distinctive legal features of the marriage tie now appears to be the Courts' powers to reorganise family finances when a couple splits up.[33] These are, in principle at least, greater than in the case of cohabiting couples:* the Courts cannot order one ex-partner to pay maintenance to another if they were never married, for example, and cohabitees do not have specific rights to the equivalent of the 'matrimonial' home.

While married partners live together, the Court's powers to make maintenance awards are very limited or of a type that is only rarely used.[34] Even the power to re-order finances on divorce is mitigated by the 'clean break' principle for spouses introduced in 1984, although the 'clean break' is not an overriding principle. Some of the other differences between married and cohabiting couples are not as great as may at first appear either:

All parents have a legal duty to maintain their children, whether they are, or ever were, married and the maintenance for a child paid by an absent parent is not restricted in amount just because it might benefit the caring parent. It may, in fact, include an element for the child's care.[35] So, if the absent parent is well off and there is a child, the caring parent may in effect receive maintenance for herself even though they were never married.

Similarly, although cohabiting couples do not have

*This chapter covers 'family law'. The obligation to maintain under social security law is covered in the following chapters.

automatic rights to their joint home if they split up, unless, like anyone else, they happen to jointly own it or rent it, they may nevertheless have rights if a Court decides that the intention of the couple was that it should be shared.[36]

Conclusion   Policies have responded to family change and diversity but not in any clear-cut way. Sometimes objectives have changed but sometimes it is the methods designed to achieve the old objectives which have changed.

Sometimes the policy response has benefited the people concerned but sometimes it has restricted their rights. Sometimes a wider range of relationships has been brought into the family net but sometimes the unit on which policy is based has been narrowed.

Meanwhile the institution of marriage, the essence of the model family, is not extinct as far as government policies are concerned. But it is a very different relationship in law from what some people may imagine:

Marriage is not a financial partnership. Each can act separately and own their own property; they can own things jointly but so can other people; and, while the marriage lasts under one roof, it is very difficult to establish a legal right to maintenance.

Chapter 2

The 'benefit' family

What is the 'benefit family'?

To what extent does the model family described in the previous chapter underly the present social security system? The married couple with husband as breadwinner and wife as homemaker and childrearer was undoubtedly the model around which the Beveridge Plan was constructed, although bachelors and spinsters were catered for as well.[37]

The present system, on the other hand, also pays attention to those 'living together as husband and wife' and, in some cases, to extended families and 'quasi' family relationships as well. Before examining why, it is important to note an important fact about the benefit system, which is that almost any generalisation about it can be refuted. This is as true of the way that it defines the family as it is of its other aspects.

The reason is partly that the so-called benefit 'system' is not a single system at all but is made up of several subsystems which recognise family and other relationships in different ways. These can be classified into three:

• Contributory (National Insurance) benefits

• Means-tested benefits

• Categorical benefits (paid for certain categories of people regardless of contributions or means)

These 'sub-systems' are in turn only semi-coherent. Different benefits within each often apply different rules and take relationships into account in different ways. There are also some benefits which cannot easily be placed in any of these categories. These include employer-administered benefits for sickness and maternity, which have recently been hived off from the contributory system. There is also a distinct set of industrial injuries benefits.

Alongside all of this are the private sector occupational and personal pensions schemes, which are not normally classified as state benefits, but which are nonetheless regulated by legislation. Private sector schemes also cover other areas, such as sickness and maternity.

If family and other relationships were ignored altogether, that would also be relevant to the way that the benefit system defines the family. This paper will therefore cover benefit units in general, whether they be the individual, family, household, or something else.

In addition to the divisions already mentioned, the system is complicated by the fact that many benefits use different units at different 'stages' of the claiming process and these 'stages' can be categorised into at least four:

- **The claim**
  Who is entitled to make the claim

- **Entitlement**
  Who is taken into account by the various rules of entitlement (which may not be the same for each rule)

- **Coverage**
  Who the benefit payment is intended to cover

- **Payment**
  Who is entitled to receive the payment

For example, only one person in a couple can claim Income Support for the couple and receive the payment. But the income and needs of both are taken into account and, if one has a full-time job, neither is entitled to claim. The relevant unit at the first and last stages is therefore different from the one used at the second and third stages.

Access to a benefit may also be influenced by the rules and practices which govern methods of payment. For example, if a benefit is paid directly into a bank account, the evidence suggests that the money is more likely to be controlled by the man in a couple than if it is picked up at the Post Office and treated as part of the housekeeping money.[38]

Equally important are assumptions which are not explicitly set out in the rules but which arise because of gaps in the benefit system or inadequate levels of payment, often due to policy makers' views about family obligations. For example, although adult children and their parents are independent units, in practice the level of benefit for residential care is too low, so that many elderly parents cannot afford it unless their children contribute (see Chapter 3).

In summary, the 'benefit' family is really several families; there is not one definition but many. Indeed various definitions can apply to the same benefit. Details are set out in the Appendix. The rest of this chapter provides a summary and overview.

The 'Beveridge' family In order to understand the definitions of the family in use today, it is necessary to understand the rules and principles on which the system is grounded. This means tracing it back to its origins in the 1942 Beveridge Plan for, in spite of, or perhaps because of, the fact that the system now departs from the Plan in numerous ways, it is otherwise impossible to form a coherent picture.

The scheme presented in the Beveridge Report was based on the central assumption that full-time paid work was, and ought to be, the primary means of distributing income. This basic employment principle, interpreted in various ways, was accompanied by a number of assumptions about who was, and ought to be, financially dependent on whom. From these two sets of assumptions, the 'Beveridge' family was made.

The main benefits of the system were to replace earnings, not to subsidise them, which entailed a rigid dividing line between employment and no employment; they were only to be paid in situations where there was an acceptable reason for not being in a paid job; and they were only for people with an employ-ment record, which was to be measured by the National [39] Insurance contributions that they had paid.

There was to be no test of income, although there was also to be a separate means-tested fall-back system of National Assistance for situations which the main scheme did not cover. But this was hardly discussed in the Report and a similarly minor role was assumed for any additional voluntary insurance.

The Family Allowance was a separate type of benefit which was to cover the cost of a child regardless of parents' income, although parents' wages were expected to be high enough to cover the cost of the first child.

Housing costs were a problem which Beveridge's Plan acknowledged but left unresolved. This was partly because it was difficult to devise a benefit within his universalist framework which would cover the wide variation in housing costs for equivalent housing.

The situations covered, such as unemployment and old age, did not directly include 'caring' in any form. Like housewives, those looking after a child or a disabled person were generally expected to receive an income second-hand through a breadwinner. Widowed mothers were covered, but only through their late husbands' contributions.

Breadwinners were generally expected to be men. Although spinsters could earn their entitlement to benefit in a way similar to bachelors (but even here there were differences), they were expected to give up employment when they married. If they continued in a job, they were subject to specific rules for married women which were in several ways less favourable than the rules for their husbands.

Entitlement to benefit through a breadwinner was generally to depend on marriage. Although an addition for a 'dependent' adult was in some circumstances provided for, widows benefits and pensions were only available to women who were married.

This emphasis on marriage was two way. On the one hand, it excluded certain people, such as cohabitees, divorced women and lone parents, and, on the other, it did not draw any distinction between the function of housewife and the function of caring for a child or disabled person.

In summary, the Beveridge Plan was based on two types of unit, unmarried individuals, whose entitlement was based on their own contributions and married couples, whose entitlement was generally based on the man's contributions. These units were inextricably linked to the principle that benefit entitlement should be based on employment, with no direct recognition of caring, and to the assumption that married couples would divide their labours in such a way that men would be the breadwinners and women the carers.

The present structure

With a few exceptions of detail, the Beveridge Plan was set in motion in 1948. Although the force of the ideas embodied in it can still be felt, the structure of the system, and the place of state benefits within the overall structure of provision, look very different now.

This structural shift has arisen partly because of deliberate policy decisions to limit the National Insurance benefits.[40] But it has also resulted from social changes, such as those described in Chapter 1, which have increased the numbers of people living in situations for which the Beveridge Plan did not cater.

Means-tested benefits for those under pension age have grown out of all proportion to what Beveridge intended. Despite its name, the "Reform of Social Security" in the mid-1980s, with its Green Papers, White Paper and ensuing legislation, was almost entirely concerned with the means-tested benefits. It thus consolidated their growth and focused public attention on them as the centre of the system.

National Assistance, reformed, renamed twice, and now called Income Support, has, together with Housing Benefit, been the major cause of this growth. However, Family Credit and two categorical benefits designed to plug gaps in the contributory National Insurance system, have, to a small degree, also contributed to the shift.

In spite of all these developments, the National Insurance benefits take up just over half of public expenditure on benefits and the Department of Social Security still describes them as the centre of the state system.[41] This is largely due to the number of pensioners, of which there are over 9 million. (The next most common National Insurance benefit is Invalidity Benefit, of which there are just over 1 million recipients.)[42]

Estimated expenditure in 1990-91 was broken down between the three main groups as shown below.[43]

N.I. Benefits	55%
Means-tested benefits	24%
Non-contributory benefits	16%
Administration	5%
Total Expenditure	100%

The importance of different types of benefit varies substantially from one group of people to another. The following table shows the proportion of different groups receiving Income Support.

Elderly	16%
Unemployed	77%
Lone Parents	68%
Short term sick	11%
Long term sick or disabled	24%

The total numbers in each group are based on those receiving benefit of some kind which is not the same as the total population in each group receiving Income Support. However, as the majority of each of these groups does receive some benefit, the figures give a rough, although not perfect, indication of the importance of Income Support for different groups in 1990-91.[44]

In addition, occupational and personal schemes have become much more common than in Beveridge's day. For example, in 1988, nearly two thirds of full-time male employees were members of a pension scheme in their currrent job, as were just over half of the female full-timers,[45] but only 12% of female part-timers. These figures do not indicate how much pension people will eventually earn but they do suggest that the private sector plays more than the marginal role that Beveridge envisaged.

Employment and caring today

The founding principle that people should earn their living and their benefits through paid work remains central to the benefit system. But it has been modified. This is partly because different benefits apply the principle in different ways and partly because some 'carers' can qualify for benefit directly rather simply through their own, or their spouse's employment.

National Insurance benefits have retained the link with employment through the contribution conditions (although these differ from the Beveridge Plan in ways which are not covered here). Indeed, for the unemployed, links with employment have been strengthened in that they now have to be 'actively seeking' as well as 'available for' employment.

However, time spent out of employment 'caring' may now help to entitle an individual to a pension. This is because of 'Home Responsibilities Protection' for people bringing up children (and certain people caring for a severely disabled adult) and the pension credits provided to those receiving Invalid Care Allowance.

Although these credits and waivers cannot by themselves entitle someone to a pension, they now apply to anyone carrying out the caring functions, regardless of their marital status and thus represent an important departure from the Beveridge Plan.

Of the means-tested benefits, Income Support is the only one which, like the National Insurance benefits described here, aims to cover basic living expenses except for housing. It is only paid to those without a full-time job and applies this principle more strictly than the National Insurance system does.

Like all the means-tested benefits, it is based on the concept of 'need' and is not related to a person's previous work record. But 'need' is not enough. There is a general rule, like the condition for Unemployment Benefit, that claimants have to available for, and actively seeking, employment. However, there are some important exceptions:

Partners of claimants are exempt from the 'availability for work...' condition simply by virtue of being partners. There is also a list of exceptions which includes some forms of 'caring', such as a lone parent with a child under 16, someone looking after a severely disabled person, and various temporary situations, such as looking after a sick child or partner.

Like the pensions' credits and waivers, these are important ways of enabling 'carers' to qualify directly rather than through a partner or through their own employment. However, in the case of Income Support, if they do have a partner, they may be disqualified (see 'Who depends on whom today' below).

Family Credit's link to employment is different again. It is only available to families with at least one parent in a full-time job and therefore contravenes the Beveridge principle that benefits are to replace earnings rather than to subsidise them. Housing Benefit can also be paid to those in full-time or part-time jobs as well as to those without one. However, as a benefit for specific costs, it might be regarded as less of a break with the Beveridge pattern.

In practice, very few employed people claim Housing Benefit and only 5% of Family Credit recipients are dual earner couples. It is therefore primarily in respect of lone parents (4 out of 10 of all Family Credit recipients)[46] that Beveridge's assumed division of labour between 'carer' and 'breadwinner' is contravened.

The two categorical benefits, Severe Disablement Allowance and Invalid Care Allowance do not require a direct employment link of any kind and the latter is specifically for carers. However, when they were introduced in the 1970s, there were special rules for married women which either excluded them altogether, as in the case of ICA, or made it more difficult for them to qualify, as in the case of SDA (which was then Non-contributory Invalidity Pension and Housewives Non-contributory Invalidity Pension).

So, although they discarded contribution conditions, they excluded or discouraged one of the largest groups of people who were likely to be out of the labour force and therefore unable to fulfil the contribution conditions. These overtly discriminatory rules have now been abandoned and the majority of both SDA and ICA claimants are women, that is roughly 60% and 80%, respectively.[47]

However, these two benefits do not present as much of a challenge to the old employment principle as might at first appear. They only cover extreme circumstances where it is widely accepted that people cannot take a full-time job. But, just in case a claimant should think of doing so, the rules of SDA say that the claimant must be 'incapable' of work and ICA bans 'gainful employment', which makes them similar to other earnings-replacement benefits.

Perhaps the most significant fact of all is that they have been paid at rates below subsistence (defined as Income Support levels). Younger SDA claimants now receive more but the rate of ICA is the same as the spouse's addition paid with Invalidity Benefit. This means that it implicitly assumes that carers will receive financial support from someone else.

Child Benefit, also paid at rates below subsistence, is not only the major categorical benefit but, in that it is paid for virtually all 12 million children, also one of the major benefits of the whole social security system. Because it is designed to cover the child, it is paid regardless of the parent's employment status. The same applies to One Parent Benefit which is paid for the first child in a lone parent family.

However, as far as the child is concerned, there is an implicit earnings-replacement aspect because children under 16 have to be at school and cannot by law take a full-time job. This aspect is more explicit once school-leaving age is reached because those aged 16-18 are only covered if they are in full-time, secondary education and have therefore not entered the labour force.

A part-time solution? Given the importance of employment as a condition for receipt of benefit and the reluctance to give caring the same status as employment, the rules relating to part-time employment are particularly relevant to 'carers' if they are to be entitled to an income in their own right rather than through a 'partner'.

In theory, the recognition of 'caring' within the benefit system could take various forms. For example, the rigid line between employment and no employment could be retained so that 'carers' have to be out of employment, like unemployed and sick people, in order to receive benefit. Alternatively, it could be assumed that 'caring' will be combined with employment.

The latter option could simply mean that 'carers' were expected to work full-time like anyone else in which case the purpose of the benefit would be to recognise the extra costs of caring. No such benefit exists. Alternatively, it could mean that the benefit rules were adapted to part-timers, who are, to a limited extent, recognised under current rules, although these are not necessarily specifically designed for carers.

First, some benefits can be combined with full-time or part-time employment. Apart from Child Benefit, One parent Benefit and Housing Benefit, which can all be combined with full or part time or no employment, widows have been able to earn as much or as little as they like. Since October 1989, so can pensioners.

Second, the earnings disregards are a concession to part-time employment, although their level varies substantially between different types of claimant. For example, recipients of disability benefits are allowed £35 a week of 'therapeutic earnings' but a single Income Support claimant unemployed for less than two years is only allowed £5 a week.

Among carers, lone parents receiving Income Support are allowed to earn up to £15 net a week before their benefit is reduced £ for £; lone parents receiving Housing Benefit can earn up to £25 a week net before benefit is withdrawn at the usual rate; and, from April 1991, ICA recipients can earn up to £30 net a week before they are disqualified. Unlike the lone parent disregards, the last is net of work expenses, which makes it even higher.

Third, the rules relating to spouses of non-means-tested benefit claimants are generally more favourable to part-time work. In contrast to the basic £5 disregard which generally applies to the partners of Income Support claimants, spouses of National Insurance and Categorical benefit claimants can earn up to about £40 a week net of work expenses while their spouse claims an addition for them.

Fourth, the White Paper, 'Children Come First'[48] proposes to reduce the definition of full-time employment to 16 hours a week for Family Credit claimants. This means that claimants still have to be employed full-time but the definition is much lower than the current 24 hours, which was itself lower than the 30 hours which applied to couples before 1988. The reason given in the White Paper is that the new rule is intended to enable a parent to take and fetch a child from school while holding a job.[49]

A similar rule will apply to a proposed benefit for disabled people working 16 hours a week.[50] But this is not a comprehensive trend. The rules of Unemployment

Benefit, for example, which were always designed so that it should *not* be combined with part-time, let alone full-time, employment as a permanent way of life, have recently been tightened up.[51]

Fifth, the rules for credits and Home Responsibilities Protection towards the retirement pension apply to those who are out of employment or to those with earnings below the threshold for making contributions. This means that they are compatible with some part time earnings, and, although the limit is not high, it is higher than most of the earnings disregards.

However, credits and Home Responsibilities Protection do not generally entitle 'carers' to the short term benefits. For example, a woman who has been bringing up a child and doing a small amount of work with earnings below the threshold for making contributions would not be entitled to Unemployment Benefit if she loses her job.

Part-time earnings above the threshold are just like full-time earnings as far as qualifying for the basic pension is concerned. However, for SERPS purposes, pension entitlement may be higher if a 'carer' stays out of employment for some years than if they take a part time job with earnings above the threshold. In that sense, this particular form of protection discourages part-time employment.

Who depends on whom today

Like the 'Beveridge' family, today's 'benefit' family depends not only on assumptions about employment but also on assumptions about who is, and ought to be, dependent on whom. These also vary according to the type of benefit:

National Insurance

As Beveridge intended, benefits paid for the dependants of an individual are not related to the level of that individual's contributions and therefore introduce an element of the 'need' philosophy into the contributory system. A dependant, however, is stricly defined.

As far as adults are concerned, marriage still matters. In particular, only married couples, or, in certain circumstances, those who have been married, can gain entitlement to benefits through a partner. Divorce is recognised but only to a limited extent, which is partly why so many lone parents now rely on means-tested Income Support.

Divorced women are not entitled to widows benefits, although they can substitute at least some of their former spouse's contributions for their own in order to qualify for the basic pension. However, unlike widows and widowers, they are not entitled to a share of the other's SERPS, and the sums involved in such cases may be much larger.

Divorce after pension age is treated differently. Women who were receiving the Married Woman's Pension become entitled to a full rate pension if they divorce; and if the man remarrries, he entitles his new wife to benefit — one of the rare situations where the benefit system will pay for more than two adults in the 'family'.

Additions for an adult are generally only available for a married partner, but an equivalent addition may be paid instead for an adult looking after a child for whom the claimant receives Child Benefit. In this way, an addition may be payable for a cohabiting partner, including a homosexual one, although such partners are not explictly recognised by the rules.

Cohabitation does enter into the rules — negatively — as far as widows below pension age are concerned, in that their benefit is stopped if they cohabit. However, there is still a distinction between cohabitation and marriage as the stoppage is temporary for widows who cohabit and permanent for those who remarry.

Within marriages, most of the differences between men and women have been removed. However, there are still about one million married women who have not yet retired who are paying reduced contributions[52] known as 'the Married Women's Option' and there is no male equivalent of the Married Woman's Pension, or of Widowed Mother's Allowance.

Additions for children are no longer payable to those below pension age except with Widowed Mother's Allowance and Invalidity Benefit. (There is also a Guardian's Allowance which is not covered here.) However, even where they are payable, there is a limit on how much a spouse can earn — a rule which was introduced at the time that married women became entitled to claim additions for children.

Living in one household is not as crucial for receiving additions to National Insurance benefits as it is in the case of the means-tested ones. For example, additions for a separated spouse or child living elsewhere may be available if the claimant supports them financially, and the Married Woman's Pension is available to women living apart from their husbands.

The Married Woman's Pension has one particularly distinctive feature. Although it is based on the man's contributions, it is paid to the wife even when the husband is alive and the two live together. It is paid at the same rate as an addition for a spouse and therefore can be considered as an addition, which, unlike the others, is paid directly to the dependant.

Means-tested benefits The definition of a 'family' for means-tested benefit purposes is set out in law. But the 'liable relative', 'non-dependant' and polygamous marriage rules, as well as the provisions for carers, mean that, in some circumstances, a wider range of relationships is taken into account than the defined 'family'. What happens inside this 'family' also varies from one benefit to another.

This 'family' includes lone parents, married and cohabiting, heterosexual couples, with or without children (except for Family Credit purposes where it must include a dependent child). Once judged to be a couple, neither member can qualify independently and the means-tests apply in various ways to the income and capital of both, as well as to any children.

However, the needs of partners and children are also taken into account, and the children do not need to be related to the claimant, as long as s/he is responsible for them. But they do all have to be living in the household of the claimant in order to be included, both in the means-test and for extra payments.

In addition, for Income Support purposes, if either member of a couple has a full-time job, they are both disqualified from claiming. Even if both qualify, only one can make the claim and receive payment, although they can choose which one it is to be.

Similarly, only one can make the claim and receive payment for Housing Benefit. Community Charge Benefit is different, however. Although it is also the rule that only one of a couple can make a claim, the benefit is split between them and paid to each separately.

Couples applying for Family Credit normally have to make a joint application in that they both have to sign the form. But this is treated by the DSS as a claim from the woman and the payment is normally made to her. The man is usually shown as alternative payee but his name can be removed if the woman requests it in writing.

The separate 'liable relative' rules, on the other hand, which apply to Income Support, do not at the moment affect entitlement directly. However, as the 'liable relative' has to maintain the other relative if the latter makes a claim for Income Support, the maintenance payment may affect entitlement indirectly by raising the claimant's income. In future the effect may be more direct as the Government proposes to introduce a deduction from benefit if a lone parent does not reveal the absent parent's name.[53]

One feature of the present rules, which was only introduced in 1990, is that the DSS now has the power to recover the amount of Income Support paid for the lone parent/childcarer from the 'liable relative', even if the parents were never married or are divorced. Previously, it was just the amount paid for the child that could be recovered in such situations.

This reinforces the possibility of double dependence for a lone parent as a new partner's income and employment status is taken into account if the lone parent should try to claim Income Support, on the implicit assumption that he maintains her. Yet the former partner is liable to maintain the child and the child's carer.

The formula for drawing up the maintenance bill to be enforced by the proposed Child Support Agency also assumes that the 'absent' parent will pay for the 'caring' parent. Recourse to this Agency is to be compulsory, not only for Income Support but also for Family Credit (introducing double dependence there as well), which was not in the past covered by the 'liable relative' rules.

For Housing Benefit purposes, there are special rules relating to people living in the household of a claimant on a non-commercial or quasi-family basis. These people are called 'non-dependants', although they could equally be called 'non-independants' as they are not allowed to claim Housing Benefit in their own right and the rules assume that they pay the claimant a set amount towards housing costs.

A similar situation arises in relation to the Severe Disability Premium, which is not payable if the severely disabled person lives in someone else's household as a 'non-dependant' because it is assumed that the householder is 'caring' for the disabled person, regardless of whether such care is provided or not.

Categorical Benefits (paid without means-test or employment test) Additions for a spouse and children are payable with the two categorical benefits, Severe Disability Allowance and Invalid Care Allowance, according to rules adapted from the National Insurance benefits, although there are some differences of detail.

ICA has special features in that it is a benefit for carers and therefore includes rules relating to the cared for person. S/he need not be related to, nor live in the same household as, the claimant, but must be in receipt of a specific benefit called Attendance Allowance. ICA claimants who also need to claim Income Support are entitled to a Carer's Premium.

Where it is the 'cared for' person who receives Income Support, the interaction with the Severe Disability Premium has to be considered. This is paid at the same rate as ICA and is not payable if someone else is getting ICA on the disabled person's account. This means that the cared and the cared for have a choice — or a conflict of interest — over which one should claim.

Child Benefit is paid for every child but not to the child. The person claiming on behalf of the child does not have to be a parent but must be responsible for the child. There is a priority list of people who can receive the payment and this also determines who is to receive protection for pension contribution purposes. In practice, it is usually the mother, although in couples, the arrangements for making the payment are similar to Family Credit.

The priority list is one way in which family relationships are acknowledged for Child Benefit purposes. Another is the new (since April 1991) higher payment for the first child in a family. The extra amount is in effect like the Income Support Family Premium which is paid to all families with children but does not vary in amount with family size. It simply recognises the existence of a child.

Conclusion   In conclusion, the National Insurance benefits still enable both members of a married couple who divide the 'breadwinner and carer' functions to qualify through the breadwinner. This need not be the man, although some inequalities remain between a male and a female who is the sole breadwinner in a couple. With the notable exception of the Married Woman's Pension, and, of course, survivors benefits, claims and payments in such cases are made by, and to, the breadwinner.

At the same time, these benefits also enable married couples who are both breadwinners to qualify independently for themselves on more or less equal terms. And if they do so, the two benefits added together are higher than if they were a sole breadwinner couple, as the latter only receive 1.6 times the rate for an individual.

Couples receiving means-tested benefits have no such option. The entitlement of one partner is firmly linked to the income, and sometimes also the employment status, of the other. Who can make the claim and receive the payment varies from benefit to benefit but all the means-tested benefits add together the needs and resources of couples and children who live together. Unlike the National Insurance benefits, this includes heterosexual cohabiting, as well as married, couples.

Entitlement to the categorical benefits is mostly based on the individual, with the obvious proviso that there has to be a 'cared for' person somewhere in order for a 'carer' to qualify for ICA. Claims and payments are therefore also made by, and to, the individuals entitled to benefit, except in the case of Child Benefit, where someone has to be entitled for the child.

All these benefits are based on the assumption that paid employment is, and ought to be, the primary means of distributing income, although this principle is applied in various ways. It has now been modified by some recognition of caring responsibilities and by tentative steps to enable benefit recipients to combine these responsibilites with employment.

Overall, the recognition of 'caring' has been limited. Caring for a child does not, of itself, entitle a person to a benefit at the time unless s/he is a lone parent or the child is sick or disabled. However, the indirect recognition of past 'caring' for pension purposes is an important means of enabling women (and men) who have spent time out of the labour force bringing up children or caring for a disabled adult to qualify for a pension in their own right.[54]

Chapter 3

Changing Directions

Chapter 2 has described what the 'benefit' family means today. This chapter looks to the future. But it does this first by examining past trends in the 'benefit' family to see if they provide any pointers. It then quotes major official statements about reform and finally sets out what it would mean to develop the definition in a wider or narrower direction.

Trends in the 'Benefit' family: A story

To some extent, Chapter 2 already gives an indication of past trends, but the focus was on understanding the system today, even though a quick snapshot of the Beveridge Plan was also considered necessary. Is it possible to say more about the way that the system is going? For example, is it moving towards individual entitlement or reinforcing family ties?

Given the complexities described in Chapter 2, it is very hard to provide a summary answer to this question. It would depend on many different factors, including the balance between the National Insurance, means-tested and categorical benefits, the unit used at each stage of the benefit process, as well as assumptions about financial dependence and resource sharing within families and other units.

The way that such factors interact can be encapsulated in the story of payments for maternity expenses.[55] These were not described in the last chapter because they are payments for one off expenses rather than a benefit towards regular weekly living costs. But they typify much of what has happened to the benefit system.

In the Beveridge Plan, the Maternity Grant only covered part of the cost of maternity because this was "a reasonable and natural claim on the husband's earnings."[56] This 'natural claim' was emphasised by the fact that a married woman's entitlement was based on her husband's contributions, although employed married women could claim on the basis of their own if the husband's were insufficient.

Beveridge was not sure whether the unmarried mother should be entitled to claim at all, because he felt that this was not a situation that the benefit system ought to encourage. In the event, she was able to claim on the basis of her own contributions. But, like other National Insurance benefits, the contributions of a cohabiting partner did not count.

In this way, lone mothers and cohabiting women were excluded unless they had recently been in a job which enabled them to fulfil the contribution conditions. Divorced women were only included on their husband's contributions if the divorce was close to the birth.

This situation continued for several decades and during the 1970s it was estimated that about 10% of births were excluded. Some of these were likely to be to the poorest mothers, which led to pressure on the government for the benefit to be made non-contributory. It eventually was — in 1982 — when it became payable to all pregnant women, including those under 16 years old.

Meanwhile, a lump sum for maternity expenses had been available as a separate benefit for those claiming Supplementary Benefit(SB). Before the 1980 Social Security Act came into effect, this payment was entirely discretionary. Afterwards, although the rules did not guarantee payment in every case and the payment could vary in amount, they gave claimants rights in certain situations.

As an SB payment, this meant that women living in married couples or with a partner 'as husband and wife' could be disqualified, not only because of their own, but also because of their partner's income, on the implicit assumption that his income would be shared.

In addition, until 1983, only the man in a couple could make the claim for SB on behalf of the couple. There followed a short period when some choice was allowed but the rules for deciding who should be the claimant were extremely complicated. Since 1988, when SB became Income Support, if both partners in a couple qualify, they can choose who shall be the claimant. This does not generally affect the overall level of payment but it does affect who gets it.

However, a new rule, introduced as a consequence of allowing choice, prevented the claimant's partner from holding a full-time job. This could disqualify the couple, and the proposed reduction in the definition of full-time work from 24 to 16 hours will make this more likely.

As for maternity expenses payments themselves, the Maternity Grant was abolished in 1987 after five years as a categorical benefit. Maternity expenses grants are now only available through the Social Fund to Income Support and Family Credit claimants, although they are automatic in such cases and the payment is for a set amount.

The new rules exclude the lone mother under 16 years old, although her parents may be able to claim maternity expenses in respect of her baby if they are themselves receiving Income Support or Family Credit. They also exclude all those women whose partner's income places the couple above the limits for Income Support or Family Credit, regardless of the actual financial arrangements between them.

Trends in the 'Benefit' family

This story does not typify everything that has happened, however. Contrary to the picture that it provides, there have been some moves towards using the individual as the unit. Drawing on examples which have been explained more fully in Chapter 2, these include the phasing out of the Married Women's Option (to pay lower contributions which do not earn them a pension) and the introduction of Home Responsiblities Protection (so that some years spent childrearing eg do not damage pension entitlement).

The growth of occupational and personal pensions, as well as the introduction of SERPS, can also be seen as moves in the opposite direction. These are largely based on the individual, except for the provisions for 'survivors' (eg a widow) to inherit the pension.

The introduction of Statutory Sick Pay and Statutory Maternity Pay can also be seen as moves in the opposite direction. These were hived off from the National Insurance system during the 1980s, and no longer include additions for dependants. The same can be said of the cutback in widows benefits in 1988, which was justified by the government partly on the grounds that younger widows no longer need to be treated as dependants.[57]

The introduction of the Community Charge, although itself based on the individual, did not have as much of an impact on the structure of the benefit system as might be expected because the rebate was still subject to the 'family' means-test. It did, however, introduce 'individual' elements, in that the payment was split between each individual in a couple, and it reduced the size of the Housing Benefit non-dependant deductions, which used to include an element for rates as well as rent.

On the other hand, in accordance with the picture presented in the maternity expenses story, there has been a shift to means-tested benefits for those below pension age, which reinforces the assumption of 'family' dependence.

There have also been other changes which reinforce the financial dependence of one person on another outside the means-tested unit. These include, for example, recent changes to the 'liable relative' rules and the proposals contained in the White Paper, 'Children Come First'.[58]

But perhaps the implicit assumptions about family dependence and obligation which have the most dramatic impact on widening the unit are those which arise from 'gaps' in the benefit system rather than the rules relating directly to particular relationships.

The level of Income Support for elderly people who need residential care is one example. In 1990, the House of Commons Social Services Committee estimated that there was an average shortfall of £30 a week or more, which put a great deal of pressure on adult children, other relatives or friends to meet the difference.[59]

Other examples include the abolition of Income Support for most 16 and 17 year olds, the lower rate for the single childless aged under 25[60] and the Severe Disability Premium, which is lost if the claimant moves into someone else's household as a 'non-dependant'.

However any benefit which is paid at an inadequate level can create a 'gap'. One example is the Invalid Care Allowance which is paid at the same rate as the addition for a dependant, and, more generally, there is evidence that some families receiving Income Support are having to turn to relatives for everyday living expenses.[61]

Official attitudes   Many of the changes which have affected the definition of the 'benefit' family have arisen as a by-product of wider objectives and have not necessarily been explicitly justified in terms of the unit or units used. Nevertheless, there have been occasions when the benefit units have been the focus of attention.

The last time that such questions were explicitly initiated by the government in this country was in the review of Social Assistance published at the end of the 1970s.[62] More recently, a new draft EC Directive on Equal Treatment[63] has again raised the question of the unit. The contents of this draft are still subject to negotiation but the attitudes of the Government and others who presented evidence have already been published in a report from the House of Lords.[64]

'Social Assistance', the name given to the 1978 DHSS review, was about Supplementary Benefit, the pre-decessor of Income Support. Its concern with the unit stemmed partly from an earlier, and then impending, EC Directive on Equal Treatment for Men and Women in Social Security Schemes which has since been implemented.

The review firmly rejected any move towards larger units, such as the household, and equally firmly rejected any move towards using the individual as the basic unit. It therefore proposed to keep the existing unit as far as possible but to consider reforms at certain stages of the benefit process.

No change was proposed to the unit for assessing income, but the individual allowed to make the claim and receive benefit, which was then the husband, could not continue if equal treatment was to be the aim. Various options were examined and the husband only rule was eventually replaced, as described above.

In relation to the household, Social Assistance said:

> "To base it [the SB scheme] on the household, which would be cheaper than the present system by making relatives of those in work ineligible, would be a reversion to the household means-test of the 1930s which had unacceptable social consequences in the splitting up of families."

And in relation to the individual:

> "Perhaps the most obvious possibility would be to allow anyone to claim Supplementary Benefit as an individual and cease to treat married or cohabiting couples as a family unit... but [we] concluded that it must be ruled out on grounds of expense and the unwarranted inequities of paying benefit to the partners of prosperous husbands or wives."[65]

The version of the draft Directive on which the House of Lords reported contained several relevant provisions. The most controversial were the suggestion that member states should consider individual entitlement as a way of achieving equal treatment and the proposal to abolish entitlements derived from, and additions paid for, a spouse. Unlike the Social Assistance review, the House of Lords Report was primarily concerned with the National Insurance benefits, Child Benefit and occupational schemes. Its conclusion was ambivalent:

"Since benefit rights derived from the insurance of a husband or wife are vulnerable to the break-up of marriage, the commmittee accept that, insofar as is practicable, it is better to substitute individual rights."

However:

"It is unlikely that, in the foreseeable future, derived entitlements can be wholly abolished without hardship resulting ... Nor would it be reasonable to expect that occupational schemes could make satisfactory provision for survivors except by way of rights derived from some-one who had been a member of the occupational scheme."

Odile Quintin, then Head of the Commission's Equal Opportunities Division, said in her evidence that:

"as long as women's and men's patterns of occupation are not completely similar, probably a combination of derived and individual rights is necessary to make the transition;"

and the Commission's memorandum suggested that this might take 40 years, Denmark being the only EC country to have adopted a system exclusively based on the individual.

The Department of Social Security's response to the House of Lords report was more forthright and stressed its oppositon to a wholescale shift towards individual entitlement. It said:

"... a system of universal individual entitlements is incompatible with the UK social insurance scheme. Moreover, within occupational schemes, survivors and dependents' benefits must necessarily be based on derived rights."[66]

Judging from these two reports, it would seem that the main question has been whether, or to what extent, benefits should relate simply to the individual. But widening the unit has occasionally been considered, for example, by extending the coverage of the National Insurance additions to cohabiting partners or other adults. The last official consideration of this issue was in 1956 when the extension of additions was firmly rejected, largely on cost grounds.[67]

More recently, the House of Commons Social Services Committee was concerned that the DSS might be planning to reintroduce a household means-test. This concern arose because the DSS had decided to base the 'poverty' figures on household income rather than benefit units. However, in its reply to the Committee, the DSS ruled out this possibility:

> "The use of household income was decided upon purely technical grounds; it does not mean that the Government have any intention of using household income as a basis for benefit receipt. The Government are therefore happy to give the assurance sought by the Committee."[68]

But there have been official hints of widening the unit in other ways. For example, Sir Geoffrey Howe recently floated the idea of:

> "securing a greater commitment from children to support their parents' welfare just as in earlier life parents have to pay for children."[69]

And, in practice, some recent changes do take a wider unit into account, as the previous section has shown.

Indeed, when the Severe Disability Premium rules were questioned in a legal battle recently fought by the Child Poverty Action Group, the DSS was quoted as saying:

> "Where someone is living with their family, we think that it is reasonable to expect that they will be receiving a degree of informal care."[70]

As the case concerned an adult disabled man living with his pensioner parents, this definition of the 'family' is wider than the means-tested 'family' and, indeed, the rules would equally apply even if the householders were not the man's parents.

Future directions   This section outlines possible future options assuming, where possible, that the benefit rules, other than those directly affecting the unit, remain unchanged. The following chapters deal with some of the issues raised. This section is simply designed to show what widening or narrowing the definition of the family might mean.

National Insurance   As explained in Chapter 2, National Insurance benefits operate under a dual set of rules which enable a married couple to be treated either as two individuals or as a couple, depending on whether they each fulfil the conditions or not.

To move wholesale over to the individual as the unit would mean that additions for spouses and children, the married woman's pension and benefits for widows and widowers would all disappear, as would the right of widows and widowers to inherit their partner's SERPS.

At the latest count there were nearly two million wives and two million widows receiving retirement pensions and about half a million widows below retirement age receiving benefit, all based on their husband's contributions. In addition there were very roughly 600 thousand men and 60,000 women claiming additions who would also lose directly.[71]

The immediate effect would therefore be to cut entitlement, particularly for married women pensioners and widows. Some of those who would lose have income and capital below the limits for means-tested benefits and would, subject to the usual conditions, therefore become entitled to these benefits, with consequences that have been described in other chapters.

More limited forms of 'individualisation' are also possible. For example, the limited coverage which exists for children could be retained or payment of benefit could be split in half (or some other proportion) and made directly to the spouse in the same way as the Married Woman' Pension is now.

To move in the other direction, that is to reinforce the existing unit or to widen it, could be interpreted in many ways. For example, cohabiting couples could be treated like married ones; the children's additions could be revived and paid at rates which, combined with Child Benefit, would exceed the Income Support rates for children; divorced people could retain rights, or partial rights, to widow/ers benefits and pensions; and additions could be paid for more than one adult.

Extending entitlement to the N.I. benefits in this way would tend to produce a shift away from the means-tested benefits as some people would no longer need to claim them.

Means-tested *benefits* If means-tested benefits were to be based entirely on the individual, each member of a couple would be able to make a claim for her/himself regardless of the other's work status, income or capital. Providing that s/he fulfilled the general rules of entitlement, s/he would be entitled to benefit in her own right.

However, under present rules, adults under pension age have to be 'available for and actively seeking employment' so that not all of those with income and capital below the limits would qualify. At the moment certain people, such as lone parents, are specifically exempt from this requirement and partners are exempt simply by virtue of being partners.

Logically, the status of lone parent would disappear as there would be no couples from which to distinguish them. This could either mean that they would also have to be available for employment or that there would be new rules to exempt all those with full-time childcare responsibilities.

Total individualisation would also mean that the 'liable relative' rules, payments for children and family-related extras, such as the Family and Lone Parent Premiums, would all disappear, although income and capital belonging to the children would not affect their parents' entitlement to benefit either.

However, as in the case of the N.I. benefits, individualisation need not be total. For example, cohabiting couples, but not married ones, could be treated as individuals; various exemptions could be retained or introduced at different benefit stages, for example, to enable lone parents to be exempt from the 'available for employment' condition.

There are several options which would retain the joint means test while introducing elements of individualisation. For example, payment could be split, as is now the case for Community Charge Benefit; the earnings disregards could be reformed to enable the partners of claimants to earn more; each partner might be allowed to claim independently but also required to be available for employment.

These and some proposals which explicitly aim to reinforce the existing unit by strengthening the rights of individuals within it are difficult to categorise. Do they represent a move towards the individual basis of entitlement or do they reinforce the 'family' unit?

The proposals for treating certain benefits as 'community property' are one example.[72] Claims and payments would be made jointly, that is both partners would have to sign the claim form and both would have to sign for benefit. The benefit could then be 'community property'.

Some proponents of this option have argued that, additionally, either spouse could be given the right to request separate payment; each could be given the right to take legal action to receive all the benefit against the wishes of the other; and, for a short period, be allowed to claim independently, like separated couples can do now. This last option would mean a separate means test for each but the DSS would then have the right to reclaim the benefit from the other partner as 'liable relative'.

There are also many different options for enforcing maintenance payments which are not necessarily the same as current proposals for a Child Support Agency. For example, the 'advance' maintenance payments which exist in some countries are effectively an extra child benefit, in that a minimum is paid to the parent with the child regardless of whether the 'absent' parent ever pays up.[73]

Paradoxically, just as narrowing the means-tested unit would be likely to widen the coverage of such benefits, so widening the unit would be likely to restrict it. This is because anyone with an income in the wider unit could disqualify the others. However, widening the unit might cover an individual who did not meet the 'available for work' condition and did not fall into one of the exempt groups. In that case it would extend coverage.

Categorical
benefits
The categorical benefits are already largely based on the individual except in terms of coverage. If this was also restricted to the individual, additions for spouses and children, which are payable with SDA and ICA, would disappear, although in practice this would affect far fewer people than in the case of the National Insurance benefits.

At the moment, entitlement to ICA is exclusively linked to the 'cared for' person's benefit entitlement. To establish some other criterion which related more to the function of caring, as has sometimes been suggested, could be viewed as a form of basing benefit on the individual, and, unlike the abolition of additions, this form would extend entitlement. Similarly, raising the level of payment to the equivalent of, say, the basic pension, could be viewed as a move towards a benefit genuinely designed for the individual.

Child Benefit is also based on the individual in the sense that it is paid for virtually every child. But greater emphasis on the individual rather than on specific family relationships might take the form of changes to the rules governing claims and payments made *on behalf* of the child. For example, instead of giving priority to the mother just because she is the mother, the person actually caring for the child might be the claimant.

Raising the level of Child Benefit so that it could replace all other payments might also be considered to be a way of making benefits for children more 'individual' in that they would then be paid regardless of parents' circumstances.

The coverage of Child Benefit could also be varied in order to pay more attention either to the individual child or to family composition. For example, a flat rate for all children, as before April 1991, would place the emphasis on the individual child whereas a 'pro-natalist' structure with increasingly higher payments for the second, third, or even fourth, child would be a move in the opposite direction.

Various forms of split entitlement would also represent a move in the opposite direction. These could apply to Child Benefit or to ICA. For example, allowing more than one person to claim for one child, might be viewed as an option which would widen the unit of entitlement. Such splitting could also be carrried over to other types of benefit, such as the Income Support payments for children.

Conclusion This chapter has shown that the definition of the 'benefit' family does not appear to be moving in any consistent direction. However, underlying past and possible future changes may be policy objectives which, if consistently applied, would have a completely different impact on different types of benefit.

If the aim is to rein back public expenditure, that would tend to restrict the National Insurance family definition but to extend or reinforce the means-tested one. For example, recognising cohabitation within the National Insurance system would extend the coverage of the scheme and cost more. But, within the means-tested scheme, it is the abolition of the cohabitation rule which would extend entitlement and cost more.

Chapter 4

Models and reality

In the light of the social and economic changes reviewed in Chapter 1, how does the 'benefit' family appear? Has it sufficiently adapted to reality or does it need to be reformed?

This chapter discusses issues which have arisen because the 'benefit' family may be out of touch with the way that people live today. Because there are many such issues, this chapter concentrates on an illustrative, but central, few. They are examined under the following headings: 'sharing resources', 'the nature of the relationship', and 'employment patterns'.

Sharing resources

Several benefits make assumptions about sharing resources. Such assumptions are most obvious in the case of the means-tested benefits where the needs and resources of the 'family' are added together in order to determine the level of benefit.

Other examples include the reduction in the level of a claimant's Housing Benefit because of others living in the household, the help that adults living in the same household as a severely disabled person claiming Income Support are expected to provide, and the expectation that relatives will make up the 'gap' between the cost of residential care and the level of benefit for those who need it.

The fundamental point about all these situations is that the assumption is made regardless of what the reality may be. Other cases are not treated in the same way. For example, if a sister makes regular payments to a brother and he tries to claim Income Support, these payments will be taken into account. But it is not assumed that she makes such payments unless she actually does and any transfers in kind, such as food, are ignored.

How do families and others share resources and what obligations do they feel towards each other? These are areas of research which are attracting increasing interest[74]. This section focuses on one example, the assumption that couples who live together and claim Income Support share their resources fairly.

Without intrusive questionning from benefit officers, in practice it would probably be very difficult to establish how resources are shared in a particular situation. That is one reason why the benefit system makes the simplifying assumption that resources are fairly shared.

It might be argued that a no-sharing assumption is more realistic than a fair sharing one. However, research evidence shows that different couples use a wide variety of sharing arrangements. Although some studies have found women whose partners gave them so little that they were better off when they split up and claimed Income Support (or its equivalent),[75] many couples pool their money in one way or another. Indeed, where there is least money, the husband is likely to hand over the whole wage or benefit for the wife to manage.[76]

This does not mean that the money is fairly shared, however. In many couples, the husband controls the supposed pool and he generally controls the size of the housekeeping allowance when that system is used. Where there is money to spare, the husband is much more likely to use it for his leisure activities than the wife is for hers.

However, one of the lessons from the research into the workings of the household is the difficulty of establishing what a fair sharing arrangement would be. It is not just a question of whether the money is split 50/50 but also whether it relates to the work and household tasks which each partner performs, who benefits from the money that is spent, how separate a life couples lead, how power is used and how self-denial is to be taken into account, given the evidence that women often 'do without' for the sake of husbands and children.[77]

However, the consequence of abandoning the fair sharing assumption and replacing it with the assumption that income is not shared at all would be to pay a benefit intended for those in need to many who do have substantial resources on which to draw.

A related, but distinct, assumption is that there are economies of scale when expenditure is made in common and consumption is shared. This is because less is then needed in order to achieve a given standard of living.

For example, the rules for determining a reasonable rent for Housing Benefit purposes allocate married and cohabiting heterosexual couples one bedroom and other adults one bedroom each; couples who are treated as a single unit only receive 1.6 times the benefit for a single person instead of twice as much; and Child Benefit now also reflects such an assumption which means that two families who become one receive less than they did as two separate families.

Undoubtedly, if expenditure is made in common, some economies of scale do exist. A two pint carton of milk costs less than two one pint cartons, for example. But, in practice, the extent of such economies depends also on the family lifestyle, such as the extent to which people buy food and cook for each other, or all eat their separate TV dinners watching their separate TVs.

Particular issues arise in relation to lone parents[80] and to children. For example, does it make a difference whether the children are the same sex? But, in general, it is probably in relation to housing that economies of scale play the biggest role. For example, how many people would expect to have one kitchen each?

However, even in relation to housing, the existence of economies depends on value judgments about lifestyles and the role of benefits. For example, if the purpose of a benefit is to provide a bare minimum in order to survive, then assuming that most couples would choose to share a bedroom, requiring them to do so might not lower their living standards as it would if two friends were required to do so.

Alternatively, if the philosophy behind the benefit stresses the rights of individuals and their ability to make choices, then the rules would be more likely to allow each individual one room with which s/he can do what s/he likes.

In summary, the fair sharing assumption represents a kind of rough justice. But it may be very rough indeed, particularly as lifestyles appear to be becoming ever more diverse. A major consequence of retaining it is that the poverty of individuals within the family goes unrecognised[78] and the assumption about economies of scale make this problem worse. However, the no sharing assumption appears to be equally unrealistic.

The nature of the relationship

One aspect of the resource sharing assumption is that it is only applied to certain types of relationship in certain situations. The joint means-test, for example, applies to married and heterosexual cohabiting partners but not to other adults.

One school of thought would retain the sharing and economies of scale assumptions but would abandon the attempt to distinguish between different types of relationship. Economies of scale would be recognised by simply paying a 'living alone' allowance but whether it would be realistic would depend on the extent to which different types of relationship really do affect the way that people live and whether it applied to Housing Benefit or to benefits for everyday living as well.

This section will focus on marriage and cohabitation as an example of the way that assumptions about relationships may not reflect reality. In particular, should they be treated in the same way as each other or are they essentially different?

The 'cohabitation rule', which treats them the same, applies chiefly to the means-tested benefits but can also affect One Parent Benefit and Widows' Benefits. It has been particularly controversial and may even create incentives for people to stay out of relationships which would deprive them of their own entitlement to benefit or reduce the total income available to the couple.

Similarly, the means-tested benefits may also discourage couples from getting married or, once married, from staying together. However, if the decision to cohabit is a more marginal one, then the influence on cohabitation is likely to be greater.

In either case, the 'disincentive-to-couples' effect depends partly on whether resources are fairly shared and whether the assumptions about economies of scale built into the system are correct. For example, if a couple really does share equally and it really does cost them 1.6 times as much as a single person to live together, then there would be no disincentive effect.

In so far as the disincentive effect exists, it is more likely to apply to a lone parent because a lone parent is entitled to benefit in her(his) own right on account of being a lone parent. A single childless person, on the other hand, has to satisfy the 'availability for work' requirement and could therefore benefit from being included in her (his) partner's claim, thus becoming exempt from the requirement.

One problem with the 'cohabitation rule' has been lack of privacy. Marriage is relatively easy to prove but the questions asked in order to establish whether a couple is cohabiting are likely to be intrusive, however sensitively they are investigated, and they are open to a wide variety of interpretations particularly in borderline cases, with 'perverse' decisions as a result.

One example, is the case of a 21 year old unemployed woman who went to live with a seriously disabled old family friend of 64. She looked after him but had her own room, her own furniture and cooked her own meals. A tribunal decided that they satisfied the 'stability' and 'financial' criteria normally used for making decisions about cohabiting couples.

However, the tribunal also decided to ignore the two criteria which the couple did not fulfil, that is the presence of joint children or of a sexual relationship. It decided that, in view of the man's state of health, they were irrelevant. The couple were therefore judged to be cohabiting. The decision was eventually overturned but it took two years.[81]

The issue of cohabitation was raised in the 1985 White Paper on the Reform of Social Security but only briefly in relation to young people between ages 18 and 25. It proposed (and this proposal has since been implemented) to cut the single person's rate of Income Support for this age group to half the rate for all couples over 18.

The effect, said the White Paper, would be that two young unemployed people with no other income living in one household would receive the same level of benefit whether they were treated as partners or not and there would be less need to enquire into whether they were cohabiting.[82]

If the cohabitation rule is regarded as undesirable, the question is whether it can simply be abandoned so that cohabiting couples would be treated like brothers and sisters or two friends, or whether it would be necessary to treat married couples as individuals as well.

The argument against abandoning it is that it would treat cohabiting couples more favourably than married ones. This, in turn, may be an argument of principle or an argument based on a view about the nature of cohabitation. If it is significantly different from marriage, then there may be a case for treating it differently.

The evidence on this is sparse,[83] although it does suggest that cohabiting couples are more likely to keep their finances separate than married ones and have different views about the relationship, although this may be due to differences in age between cohabiting and married couples (see Chapter 1).

Legally, under general family law, there are still some differences but not as many as is often supposed (see Chapter 1). Nevertheless, divorced partners without children, in particular, do have rights against each other which cohabiting partners who have split up do not.

At the moment the treatment of cohabitation often seems unfair because it is usually recognised where it will restrict entitlement and not where it would confer rights. As far as consistency is concerned, an alternative to abolishing the cohabitation rule for means-tested benefits would be to extend the additions for spouses paid with National Insurance benefits, although this might not seem appropriate if the intention is eventually to do away with the need for such additions.

After a couple has split up, there is little difference between the way that benefits treat the two types of couple, although that is because, with the exception of the basic pension, the benefit system make little positive provision for divorced couples.

However, due to the rise in divorce and the insecurity of modern marriage, it has been suggested that there should be some mechanism for ensuring that couples who have split up can share in the other's SERPS entitlement.[84] The Lord Chancellor's Department considered the issue in relation to occupational pensions in a consultative paper issued in 1985.[85] If such proposals were to be implemented, the treatment of married and cohabiting couples would no doubt become a live issue in this context as well.

The question here is not only between marriage and cohabitation but whether the loss of earnings and long-term right to pension is due to the relationship or to the fact that time has been taken out of the labour market to raise children.

In practice the two may be connected if the decision to have and look after a child would not have been taken without an understanding between the partners.[86] Against this it can be argued that the insecurity of modern marriage relationships has changed what it is realistic to expect of them and that alternative forms of compensation and/or steps to enable childrearers to earn their own entitlement to pensions are equally, if not more, appropriate, at least within the state scheme.[87]

Employment patterns

It is interesting to note that in Denmark, the only European Community country which has moved towards individual entitlement to benefits, women's participation in the labour force is almost the same as men's (although they tend to work shorter hours than men).[88] They are therefore likely to be able to earn their entitlement to benefits which are conditional on employment.

In this country, as described in Chapter 2, the assumption that the world is divided into breadwinners who earn benefits and childrearers who are dependent on a breadwinner still permeates the system. Is this a realistic reflection of current employment patterns?

The changes in women's employment patterns have been documented elsewhere[89] and are not covered in detail here. However, it is worth stating that the employment of women, including, in particular, the employment of women with children, is vastly higher than it was when the Beveridge Plan was introduced. Combined with large scale male unemployment, the result is that in recent years less than half of the employed labour force has been composed of full-time male employees.[90]

Nevertheless, as Chapter 1 pointed out, women's employment still does not resemble men's because many women take years out of the labour force to care for children and disabled relatives. They also perform a greater share of household tasks and many work part-time. Several millions have earnings below the threshold for making National Insurance contributions.[91] Although some of these may be protected for pensions purposes, they are not protected as far as many short-term benefits are concerned.

The payment of Income Support to lone parents has been a major exception to the employment basis of entitlement as there is neither a backward-looking nor forward-looking employment condition (See Chapter 2). As the numbers of lone parents have grown, there has also been a massive growth in the numbers and propotion dependent on Income Support,[92] which, to some extent reflects the fact that patterns of employment among those caring for children are not the same as those of breadwinners.

However, the benefit rules may also discourage lone parents who would like a job from taking one because earnings are deducted almost in full from Income

Support. This means that the job is not financially worthwhile unless s/he can command high enough earnings to lift her/him off Income Support altogether. For many, this is likely to mean working full-time which may be difficult for someone with child care responsibilities.

Proposed changes to the benefit rules aim to encourage lone parents into employment (see previous chapters). However, if the obstacles to the employment of women with children lie outside the benefit system, for example, in the lack of good quality child care facilities, the effect of such proposals on changing employment patterns is likely to be limited. Several studies have in fact found that many women with children would return to work sooner if suitable child care facities were available.[93]

The Married Woman's Pension also raises the question whether the benefit system discourages women from taking a job. If a woman can get a pension based on her husband's contributions worth 60% of the full pension, the return on her own contributions is less than in the case of other people, and, if she cannot earn more than the 60%, the return on her contributions is nil.

In other words, in reflecting women's weaker employment status, does the benefit system also reinforce it? Maybe people do not think about their employment in terms of their pension entitlement but a third example lies in the Income Support rules for a couple which first assume that there will only be one breadwinner and then create obstacles to any other arrangement.

The rules do allow complete role reversal. For example if a wife could earn more than the amount of benefit the husband receives for the family, it would be worth her while to work full-time and for the husband to stop claiming, assuming this were acceptable to the husband.

Unless she can command exceptionally high earnings, she would probably have to work full-time to earn more than the family's total benefit entitlement, especially if there were children in the family. This is a similar issue to the one that arises in the case of lone parents, although the rate of benefit for a couple and the amount of earnings needed are higher for a couple.

The proposed reduction in the definition of full-time employment to 16 hours a week for Income Support and Family Credit purposes may therefore have as much effect on the partners of unemployed men claiming Income Support as on lone parents, who were the focus of attention in the White paper containing the proposals.[94]

The reason that couples do not swap over the breadwinner role when the man is unemployed needs to be investigated further but evidence from one recent study suggests that it is partly to do with the employment opportunities available to women with children when the husband is employed. These still make it pay for him to be the full-time worker unless it appears to the couple that he is likely to be out of work for a very long time.[95]

The benefit system itself does not encourage partners to share employment, although it may encourage them to share unemployment. It has, indeed, been argued that the disincentive to women's employment within the Income Support rules reinforces male unemployment as well. This is because the man then has to find a job which will pay for his wife and children as well as for himself.[96]

How far do the disincentives bite in practice? It is clear from just a cursory glance at the General Household Survey, for example, that wives of unemployed men are very much more likely to be economically inactive than the wives of employed men. However, this could be for several reasons, some of which, such as the availability of jobs in the local area, may have nothing to do with the benefit system.

The evidence does, however, suggest that the wives of men on Income Support (and previously, Supplementary Benefit) are less likely to be employed than the wives of men receiving National Insurance Unemployment Benefit, where the disincentive effect is much weaker because it is only the addition which is lost if the wife has earnings above the amount allowed.[97]

Conclusion None of the assumptions considered in this chapter is wholly realistic. But neither is any single alternative. Even among families with children, the majority are not couples with a breadwinner father and a non-employed mother. But nor is the real world made up entirely of role-sharing dual-earner couples, lone parent families, or extended families sharing the child care among several family members.

Similarly, most couples appear not to share their income equally but the no-sharing assumption appears equally unrealistic; and, although some cohabiting couples may live just like married ones, others may have chosen to cohabit because they want an arrangement which is more independent than marriage.

However, by making certain assumptions which are not always realistic, the benefit system has a number of drawbacks which apply particularly to the means-tested benefits. For example:

– where couples do not share resources fairly, hardship will result for a partner who is forbidden by the rules to claim independently;

– heterosexual couples who cohabit rather than marry because they want financial independence or because the relationship is a trial one, are paid a lower rate of benefit than two single people, just as if they were married, even though the legal obligations of marriage do not apply to them and their lifestyle may not justify the economies of scale that are assumed;

– and where one partner is unemployed, treating the 'family' as a sihgle unit is likely to create disincentives for either partner to take a job.

Chapter 5 Reform

Objectives In practice, changes to the definition of the 'benefit' family have not been made for the sake of widening or narrowing the definition for its own sake. They have been made in order to achieve other objectives.

The need for reform is therefore normally judged in terms of specified objectives. But the objectives which the benefit system has tried to serve, or has had wished upon it, are varied and complex. The Government's 1990 Public Expenditure White Paper, for example, lists eleven for the system as a whole and Peter Townsend has identified seven for Child Benefit alone.

The objectives may be overlapping, interdependent, subordinate one to another or just contradictory. It is therefore not possible to draw up a simple checklist and choices have to be made. This Chapter will therefore not attempt to be comprehensive and will concentrate on issues which have arisen in particular situations.

Even a single criterion can be interpreted in many different ways. Take the elimination of poverty and equal treatment for men and women — two of the objectives which have led to concern with the 'benefit' family. Abel Smith has listed five different ways in which equal treatment can be interpreted for social security purposes[100] and the debates concerning the definition of poverty are legendary.[101]

These two objectives may sometimes conflict and sometimes overlap. Paying benefit to wives of men with jobs, for example, might in some circusmtances do little to eliminate poverty, although it might achieve equal treatment. If resources are not fairly shared within families and also if poverty is defined as deprivation in the capacity to act rather than simply as deprivation in the consumption of resources, then the two goals are more likely to overlap.

Equal treatment itself may be the goal or it may be the outcome which is important. Formal equality within the rules does not necessarily mean equality in practice. The Income Support rules, for example, now allow a couple to choose who shall be the claimant as long as each qualify. But in 1989, only 4% of women in couples receiving Income Support were in fact the claimant.

Whether this was because women in such couples did not know the rules, did not qualify, were bullied or did not think that it was worth bothering to challenge the man's 'breadwinner' status as it would not result in any extra money for the couple, the figure does not reveal. But it does suggest that, no matter what the objective may be, changing the rules, on its own, is unlikely to have much impact if underlying patterns of family life do not accord with the assumptions and objectives of the change.

It takes a unit to judge a unit

Insofar as a change to a benefit unit (or any other change to the system) is judged by its impact on people, is it the impact on the individual, the family, the household or some other unit that matters? In other words, in order to judge the need for reform, it is necessary to have a unit of analysis as well as a benefit unit.

A thoroughly scientific analysis might therefore look like a grid with the units used, or proposed, for benefit purposes along one side and the units of analysis along the other. However, given the variety of benefit units currently used, let alone the permutations and combinations that might be developed if larger units were to be taken into account, this is hardly a feasible exercise.

Nevertheless, the results are likely to be different if it is the individual or some other unit, such as generation or community, which is used when analysing the distribution of income or the extent of poverty.

For example, there is a substantial amount of social security literature on equity between generations,[104] leading to such suggestions as linking a person's pension entitlement to the number of children s/he has produced.[105] An example of the community unit can be found in Australia, where isolated Aborigine communities may now choose to have unemployment benefit paid to the community (through its leaders) instead of to individuals. However, the rights of individuals as a result of this measure have caused some concern in Australia,[106] as might some of the pro-natalist measures designed to achieve equity between generations, were they to be implemented here.

In this country, the case for using the individual as the unit of analysis has wide support even among those who would retain the 'family' as the unit for many benefits. For example, the Department of Social Security's review of the 'Low Income Families Tables' (popularly known as the 'poverty' figures) said:

> "the ideal unit might be the individual, since this would take account of the extent to which the income received by benefit units or households is actually shared between their members."[107]

However, the report then went on to say that in practice it was not possible to use the individual as the unit because the data available was not adequate to the task. In general, if it is believed that families or other units share resources, or at least, that some units share some resources to some degree, and the information about such sharing is not available, then it is also useful to know about the impact of a benefit change on this wider unit.

However, even if the family or household is often the decision-making unit for work and consumption,[108] that is, even if individual welfares are interdependent, they can be seen as distinct[109] and just because family incomes may be shared and decisions taken jointly, does not necessarily mean that some family members may not be more deprived than others.[110]

Recognising diversity The situations described in the last chapter are by no means the only elements of diversity in the way that people live today, as Chapter 1 has indicated. In addition, diversity is not simply a matter of varied patterns of family life and relationships at one point in time, it can affect one individual over his or her lifetime.

The enormous rise in divorce rates is but one indication of the fact that a stable pattern of family life cannot be assumed. The same applies to movements in and out of employment, which include full-time and part-time employment, as well as unemployment and withdrawal from the labour force.

The result is that no single definition of the family is likely to be realistic. Unless an attempt is to be made to put the clock back, which, as Chapter 1 has indicated, politicians are reluctant to do, what is needed is a benefit system which will accommodate a wide range of situations.

Nevertheless, there are bound to be differences of view about the range of situations which is acceptable. Charles Murray, for example, deplores the role of the benefit system in facilitating the growth in the number of lone parent families and the creation of an underclass — a causal conection which has yet to be proved — while others would regard existing provision for lone parents as inadequate.[111]

The wider family? One way of incorporating diversity into the benefit system is to specify many more relationships and the circumstances in which they need to be taken into account, in other words, to widen the definition of the 'benefit' family. This could mean, for example, giving divorced people a right to their previous partner's earnings related pension or extending the additions for spouses paid with national Insurance benefits to a cohabiting partner.

Extending the definition is relatively easy in situations which are very clearly defined, even if they are rare. For example, polygamous marriages which have taken place in a country which recognises polygamy are currently recognised, to a limited extent, for means-tested benefit purposes.

However, if there are very many of these situations, this approach could create an extremely complicated system and there would be particular difficulties for those categories which are difficult to define, such as cohabitation, where decisions in practice have frequently created a sense of injustice.

There is also the question of ensuring that the relationships defined in law correspond with the financial support really provided and the sense of obligation that people feel towards each other. In the case of young people aged 16-17, for example, it has been necessary to draw up a long list of exceptions for those situations where it is considered unreasonable or impossible for parents' to support them and, even so, it is uncertain whether such protection is reaching all those in need.[112]

Another possible extension of the 'benefit' family would rest on adult children's responsibility for their parents, although carrying this idea to its logical extreme by abolishing pensions seems unlikely. It would certainly undo the principle of financial independence for old people which has been an important element of public policy since pensions were introduced at the beginning fo this Century.

Yet the general idea has been floated by certain politicians and, for residential care purposes, it is already accepted that adult children (and others) may have to contribute towards the fees. However, although some families are willing to do so, the evidence on existing attitudes suggests that it may be dangerous to push this assumption too far.

Although relationships between parents and adult children are often founded on a sense of obligation, evidence suggests that this is not universally accepted and that it has definite limits.[113] Indeed, it has been argued that the introduction of old age pensions may have encouraged family ties and mutual support as old people were less likely to be viewed as a burden.[114]

There is also the question whether families have the resouces to pay, whatever they may feel about their duties. In this sense there is a difference between situations where families are not compensated for the support that they are expected to provide and those where they are.

However, in both cases, questions about personal autonomy and the desirability of treating one person as financially dependent on another may arise.[115] In some situations these may be particularly difficult to resolve, for example, in the case of someone caring for a severely disabled person, should it be the carer who receives a benefit or the cared for person so that s/he can pay for care?

Does the answer depend on whether the benefit is for the extra costs of caring and disability or whether it is designed to replace earnings?And is it possible to allow choice between carer and 'cared for' without also creating a potential conflict of interest?

These issues are more likely to arise between adults as few people would advocate paying benefits directly to children, except, perhaps in the case of young people still at school, where this has been an issue.[116] However, it is sometimes argued that certain benefits in kind, such as school meals, should be provided directly to children rather than as cash to their parents.[117]

There is also the question of who suffers. If the resources are not there and the obligation is fulfilled, then the price is likely to be hardship for the provider. Even if the resources are there, if the obligation is not fulfilled, then the price is likely to be hardship for the ones whose needs have been ignored.

In the case of young people sleeping rough in the streets, this poverty is apparent. But the argument applies in other situations, including husbands and wives who live together, and in such cases poverty within the family may be hidden from public view.[118]

It may be possible to build up the legal rights of individuals against each other in order to ensure that obligations are fulfilled. But, in practice, Court action to enforce them is difficult, sometimes costly, and the decisions may be hard to enforce.

Even in the case of child support, where it might be thought that the sense of duty was at its strongest, recent research has shown that only 1 in 3 lone parents receive money for their child.[119] As a result, the Government has felt it necessary to propose a statutory agency to ensure that such obligations are fulfilled.

This measure may be seen as a move to increase the financial dependence of one partner — most likely the woman — on the other — most likely the man, even after they have separated. Yet because it involves an outside agency, it does introduce a buffer between the two partners and may be more reliable than private means of enforcing payments.

The extent to which it enables the 'dependent' one to achieve a secure income with dignity and could thereby help towards the goal of financial independence depends on the rules under which the agency operates and the ones proposed have been highly controversial.

Similar arguments can be applied to other proposals which would extend partners' claims on each other, such as the proposals for sharing pension entitlement after divorce. These would reinforce women's financial dependence on men but might achieve a higher income for at least some of them.

However in neither of these two examples does the 'private' solution of reinforcing dependence on a previous partner solve the problem of those whose previous partner cannot afford to pay or does not have a pension worth splitting, unless there is an adequate publicly underwritten minimum. Further issues also arise in relation to those who never had a stable relationship with the previous partner.[120]

More generally, if 'freedom from the arbitrary will of another'[121] or establishing genuine interdependence are among the criteria chosen for the benefit system, then it may be necessary to concentrate on the public rather than the private solutions. However, by itself, removing dependence on another individual would not be very successful if there is no alternative source of income or if it simply results in stigmatising dependence on the state or the rule of an exploitative employer.[122] That depends on the terms, conditions and levels of payments from public sources and from employers.

The individual? Instead of widening the family definition, the opposite solution would be to move entirely to a system based on the individual. Unlike the former type of proposal, which tends to be made piecemeal in order to deal with specific problems, proposals for individual entitlement are more likely to form part of a grand design.

Perhaps the most far-reaching proposal is the 'basic income' which would be paid to all individual citizens, regardless of relationship or work status, thus presenting a major challenge to the employment basis of the system described in Chapter 2.

Many of its proponents see individual entitlement as an essential aspect of a 'basic income'[123]. However, a 'basic benefit' would face even more acutely than the present system the problem of balancing cost, level of payment and the taxes needed to pay for it. Therefore, in order to reduce the cost, some proponents have dropped the individual basis of entitlement.[124]

A more fundamental criticism arises from the fact that paid work is still the chief way in which income is distributed in this country. If this continues, and if producers continue to limit what is available to non-producers, it may be necessary to define fairly strictly those situations where employment is not expected, in order to achieve an adequate level of benefit. Nevertheless, those situations could be differently defined from the way that they are now.[125]

Instead of a thoroughgoing 'basic benefit', there are other ways in which benefits could be based on the individual. These would also help solve many of the problems discussed in this Paper, such as the hidden poverty of family members, the difficulties with the 'cohabitation rule', and the obstacles to employment created by treating couples as a single unit.

As Chapter 3 showed, in practice, the objection to removing the extra coverage provided for dependants within the National Insurance system rests largely on women's weaker labour market position which means that many do not currently qualify in their own right.

However, in the long run, many more women are likely to qualify through their own employment and, even left as they are, the National Insurance benefits are therefore relatively well adapted to making the transition. If it were thought necessary, they could even be adapted in the other direction to include extra additions in clearly defined situations, for example, to help Muslim families where there may be a strong religious objection to women's employment.

In the case of Income Support, two arguments against individual entitlement have predominated. One is that many women who do share their partner's standard of living would benefit and the other is the high cost.

As far as the former is concerned, many wealthier women, so frequently mentioned in this context, would be ruled out by the £8,000 capital limit. At current rates of interest, this is very much lower than the amount of capital that is now effectively allowed tax free under independent taxation.

As for the latter, the actual cost would depend on a number of factors, such as the numbers disqualified by the capital rule and the rules requiring claimants to be available for employment.

If it were assumed that all women with children had to be available for employment, this would reduce the cost of change but would constitute a major break with tradition and, in view of the evidence presented in Chapter 1, would probably be unacceptable.

There is also the question of partners without children. Would it be acceptable to require them to be available for work? The Australians, for example, have recently made such a change but only for those under age 21.[125] Given that it is the birth of a child and other 'caring' responsibilities which damage employment prospects rather than marriage or living with a partner, this might be acceptable here.

On the other hand, if all those now caring for children were to be exempt from the requirement, the cost would be much higher and Income Support would, among other things, become a benefit for childrearing. A number of questions would then arise. In particular, would this tend to reinforce child carers' weaker financial position in the long run by discouraging employment, even though it might protect them from extremes of hardship in the short term?

Similar questions arise in relation to other 'carers' in so far as they have had to limit their employment in order to care. (Benefits for those looking after a disabled adult raise additional issues which are not discussed here. For example, many such carers are over retirement age and not necessarily in need of a benefit to replace earnings. They might, however, be considered to need a benefit for the extra costs of caring).

If the objective were instead to ensure that there was no disincentive either to take employment or to 'stay home', a benefit for 'care' which enabled the carer either to 'stay home' or to take employment and pay for care might be considered more appropriate. In that case, issues would arise as to the form that the benefit should take. In particular, as all means-tested benefits tend to have a disincentive effect, a non-means-tested benefit might be considered more suitable.

One route out of this and other dilemnas posed by the means-tested benefits (see Chapter 4), which would also provide an alternative to the 'basic income', would be to improve access to benefits which are based on a different philosophy,[126] such as the National Insurance ones. At the moment the rules for these benefits tend to exclude some groups. Lone parents are one but anyone who has difficulty fulfilling the employment conditions could be affected.

Various ways of extending entitlement to the National Insurance benefits have been suggested, such as changing the threshold for making contributions and liberalising or abandoning the contribution conditions in favour of a less stringent work test.[127]

Improving the categorical benefits is another way – one of the most immediate suggestions being to raise the level of Invalid Care Allowance, so that it genuinely enables an individual to survive independently.[128]

Intermediate solutions, such as those designed to improve the rights of individuals within couples have also been proposed (see Chapter 3). These include raising the level of the earnings disregards, either in general or for the partner of a claimant, and extending the 'liable relative' rules to couples who live together which would enable them to claim independently.

A more limited approach would simply enable payments to be split and made separately to each partner while leaving the rules of entitlement unchanged. This is how the Community Charge Benefit works and it could be introduced as an option for other benefits. At the moment the DSS has power to make payments to a partner but is only likely to do this in extreme circumstances and it is not a right available to claimants.

This more limited approach would only split the couple rate, that is, 1.6 times the single person's rate. But it would ensure that some money reached each partner and a similar choice could be allowed in relation to provision for children, or it could be paid to the one receiving Child Benefit. There would be some extra administrative cost in allowing such choice but it is unlikely to be very great.

Conclusion This Paper has shown the complexities of the present 'benefit' family definition and touched on a wide range of issues. Among these were equal treatment for men and women, the ages at which children should be treated as adults, the responsibilities of adult children for their own parents, the potential conflict of interest between the needs of the carer and 'cared for', the difference between cohabitation and marriage and the way that living costs are shared, each of which raises distinct issues which have not all been pursued here.

However, if one theme were to be singled out, at the heart of many of the dilemmas which arise when trying to widen or narrow the 'benefit' family lies the fact that, under present rules of entitlement, caring responsibilities only qualify a person for benefit in certain limited situations.

Although the rules have changed since the Beveridge Plan, where caring responsibilities did not directly entitle people to benefit at all and where 'carers' were generally assumed to be married women who would be financially dependent on their husbands, caring responsibilities still present a challenge to the benefit system.

Indeed, it can be argued that they are more of a challenge than ever now that more unstable relationships and more fluid and flexible patterns of employment are common. Although no single model has replaced it, the breadwinner and dependant model is becoming less and less realistic.

Policies are therefore adapting, but slowly and imperfectly, either by attempting to enforce the private dependency by public means for the benefit of the dependant or by giving the 'carer' more access to benefit in his or her own right.

In view of the problems of hardship which are likely to arise where government policies assume the existence of family obligations which are in fact out of tune with current beliefs and practices, there may be limited scope for extending the definition of the benefit family.

On the other hand, while the employment basis of entitlement continues to predominate, individual entitlement would disadvantage many 'carers'. However, it could solve problems, such as the hidden poverty of family members, the 'cohabitation rule' and the obstacles to employment created by treating couples as a single unit (see Chapter 4).

Individual entitlement is also particularly suited to a world where personal relationships cannot be relied upon to provide a secure income and where a value is placed on the rights of individuals within families. The extent to which the real world does fit this picture is, of course, debatable, but as this Paper has shown, there have undoubtedly been trends in both these directions (see Chapters 1 and 3 in particular), even if some recent social security measures have attempted to reassert family obligations (see Chapter 3).

If the employment basis of entitlement does continue to predominate, individual entitlement would have to be combined with other policies designed to help 'carers' below pension age combine their responsibilities with employment. For example, if good quality child care services were available and there was good provision for people with disabilities, then many more individual 'carers' would be able to take jobs and qualify for benefits based on employment status in their own right.

However, not all 'carers' might want to do this. Evidence also suggests that there is no consensus that people with caring responsibilities *ought* to take a paid job even if it is widely believed that they should have the freedom to do so if they want to (see Chapter 1).

Specific benefits for those caring for children and disabled adults are sometimes seen as the solution, although the terms and conditions on which they would be available would be crucial and would greatly influence the cost. For example, would they only be available to women with children under a certain age?

An intermediate solution sometimes proposed is to improve the position of part-timers which might encourage part-time employment. For, in spite of some recent changes, the benefit system is still badly adapted to those who do not fit the permanent full-time work pattern.

However, benefits for part-timers raise a number of issues. On the one hand, they could be seen as giving individuals more choice to combine employment with 'caring'. On the other hand, they may contravene the old philosophy that benefits are to protect those out of employment from being forced or encouraged to take low paid, marginal jobs.

The answer to this dilemna depends partly on whether the jobs that part-timers take are 'good' jobs, or at least a route into better ones, and how amenable they are to employment protection legislation, both of which are factors which lie outside the benefit system.

Like the answers to many of the other issues raised, appropriate solutions also depend on other objectives. For example, increasing the earnings disregard for Income Support claimants might alleviate the disincentive-to-work problem (although shifting it higher up the income scale). However, it would also conflict with the traditional purpose of Income Support, which is to help those most in need. In particular, it would help those with the greatest caring responsibilities least.

If benefits for children and people with disabilities were paid at a level where the 'carer' only needed to cover his or her own cost, then movements in and out of full-time, part-time and no employment would be greatly eased, as would movements from one marital status to another.

However, paying Child Benefit at a rate at which provision for children with other benefits was no longer necessary would be extremely costly and would almost certainly raise the question of parents' responsibilities for their children in an even starker form than is the case now.

Ultimately, nearly all suggestions for reforming the 'benefit' family raise such fundamental issues, not only about the benefit system, but also about the reponsibilties of one individual for another, the respective role of State and Citizen and the importance of employment for distributing income.

Nevertheless, unless it is believed that it is possible to turn the clock back and reverse recent trends in human behaviour, the current diversity of family forms means that the functions which the 'traditional' or 'model' family were supposed to perform will have to be recognised in new ways.

Appendix: The benefit units

This outline follows the pattern discussed in Chapter 2 that is, each benefit is divided into four 'stages': the claim, entitlement, coverage, payment. As far as possible, information is up-to-date at April 1991. The entitlement of young people is only briefly mentioned as this is covered in detail in a recent FPSC publication, Young People: Growing Up In The Welfare State. In general, this Appendix should only be taken as an outline. 'Welfare rights' advice is available from the sources listed.

1 Contributory (National Insurance) Benefits

The National Insurance benefits described here are designed to replace earnings. A claimant cannot therefore get more than one at a time. This also means that one spouse cannot receive an addition for the other if the other is already receiving such a benefit in his/her own right (unless the addition is worth more, in which case the difference is paid).

Unemployment Benefit (UB)

The claim
Any individual — regardless of relationships — who fulfils the rules of entitlement can be the claimant.

Entitlement
Entitlement is based on the individual claimant's contribution record and unemployed status. Although the basic National Insurance benefits are not means-tested, the income of a spouse or other adult is taken into account if a claim for an additional payment for him/her is made.

Coverage
Payments cover the individual and an addition worth about 60% extra may be payable for a spouse *or* an adult (of either sex) caring for a child for whom the claimant receives Child Benefit. The claimant need not

live with the spouse or child carer but in that case must pay maintenance or a wage. No additions are payable for children (unless the claimant is over pension age).

Payment
The claimant receives the benefit and any addition.

Invalidity Benefit

The Claim
Any individual — regardless of relationships — who fulfils the rules of entitlement can be the claimant.

Entitlement
Entitlement is indirectly based on the individual's contribution or equivalent work record and incapacity for work. There are special rules for widows and widowers to enable them to qualify if they do not meet the usual conditions. The income of a spouse or child carer is taken into account if an addition is claimed, either for an adult or for children, although the level of income allowed is higher for a child addition.

Coverage
Payments cover the individual and additions may be payable for a married spouse or child carer (see UB). Unlike UB, additions are also payable for children but the claimant or partner must receive Child Benefit for the child. If it is the partner who receives Child Benefit, then the claimant either has to be a natural parent or, if not, eg, if s/he is a stepparent, then he must wholly or mainly maintain the child and there are rules for situations where several people maintain the child.

Payment
The claimant receives the benefit and any additions.

Retirement Pensions

Of the various retirement pensions, three are described in turn: the standard Basic Pension; the (lower rate) Married Woman's Pension; and the earnings related pension (SERPS).

The first two are known as Category A and Category B pensions respectively. The latter, which are based entirely on a spouse's contributions, are also available to widows and widowers under slightly different rules, in which case they are paid at the full rate.

The Standard Basic Pension

The Claim
Any individual — regardless of relationships — who fulfils the conditions of entitlement can be the claimant.

Entitlement
Entitlement is based on the claimant's age (60+ for women and 65+ for men) and contribution record but there are special provisions for divorced and widowed people to use part of their former spouse's record if theirs is not complete. Reduced rate contributions paid by married women (now being phased out) do not count. Caring is recognised in two ways: either by contribution credits, which apply, eg, while someone receives Invalid Care Allowance, or by Home Responsibilities protection (HRP) which reduces the years during which contributions have to be paid (although not below 20 years). HRP applies to priority Child Benefit claimants and to those receiving Income Support on grounds of caring for a severely disabled person.

Coverage
The coverage for children is similar to Invalidity Benefit. For spouses, there are notable differences, for example: i) if the wife of a pensioner is of pension age herself, the Married Woman's Pension replaces the addition and ii) even if a married woman receives a pension from her own contributions, she cannot receive an addition for her husband unless she was already getting one immediately before qualifying for the pension.

Payment
The claimant receives the benefit and any addition.

The Married Woman's Pension

The claim
Only a married woman can be the claimant.

Entitlement
Entitlement is based on the husband's contributions. Both the husband and the wife must be of pension age. This pension cannot be combined with one based on the

wife's own contributions unless, because of deficiencies in her contributions, the total is no higher than this lower rate pension. The couple must be married but they need not live together. (If the woman is divorced after reaching age 60, or widowed, different rules apply and the pension is paid at the standard rate together with any additions for children.)

Coverage
This lower rate pension only covers the married woman and, like the addition for a spouse, is worth about 60% of the standard rate basic pension.

Payment
The claimant, that is the married woman, receives the benefit.

The Earnings-related Pension (SERPS)

The Claim
Any individual — regardless of relationships — who fulfils the rules of entitlement can be the claimant.

Entitlement
Entitlement is based on the claimant's age (see standard pension), earnings and contribution record. The earnings record is based on the best 20 years of earnings. From 1999, the 'best 20 years' rule will disappear and years spent caring or bringing up a child will be recognised in a way similar to that used for the basic pension, ie, those out of a job or with earnings below the N.I. threshold for contributions will receive HRP. Only widows and widowers can receive SERPS earned by their spouse. They can inherit it in full (only half for those widowed after the year 2,000) in addition to their own, subject to a limit on the total.

Coverage
No additions are payable.

Payment
The claimant receives the benefit.

Widows' Benefits

There are two alternative weekly benefits for widows below pension age: the Widowed Mother's Allowance for those with children and the Widow's Pension for those without. The main points to note about both are set out in brief below.

The claim
Only a widow can claim. There are no equivalent benefits for widowers below pension age.

Entitlement
Entitlement is based on the deceased spouse's contributions. The widow must have been married to the deceased and must not remarry or cohabit. (The same restriction does not apply to widows over pension age receiving retirement pensions on a spouse's contributions.) Entitlement is lost altogether on remarriage but only temporarily suspended during a period of cohabitation. For the widow's pension, the widow must be at least 45 and she does not receive the full rate until age 55.

Coverage
Children's additions are payable with the Widowed Mother's Allowance (although the definition of a qualifying child is slightly different from the one used for the other National Insurance benefits).

Payment
The claimant, that is the widow, receives the benefit and any addition for children.

---

2 Means-Tested Benefits

The definition of a **'family'** is the same for Income Support, Housing Benefit and Family Credit. It includes married couples who live together and heterosexual couples who 'cohabit' (officially referred to as 'living together as husband and wife' but also frequently referred to as the 'cohabitation rule'), lone parents and/or any dependent children for whom the claimant is responsible and who live with the claimant. Couples who are divorced or separated are not a 'family'.

The definition of **'living together as husband and wife'** is not set out in legislation. In practice, a number of questions may be considered relevant, although not necessarily in a clear-cut way and some are more definitive than others. The main ones are:

are the two members of the same household?

is the relationship stable?

what are the financial arrangements?

is there a sexual relationship between them?

are they caring for a child of their union?

are they publicly aknowledged as a couple?

The definition of a **'dependent child'** is similar to the Child Benefit definition (see under Categorical Benefits below) but is narrower in requiring that the child live with the claimant. If a child spends equal amounts of time in two households, it can only be treated as part of one 'family' and if there is any doubt, it is the person who is entitled to Child Benefit who is treated as responsible for the child.

An exception to this definition of a family is a marriage celebrated in a country which recognises polygamy. This is not recognised by the National Insurance benefits but the means-tested benefits make provision for an extra payment for each partner, which is less than the extra paid for a partner in a couple.

Income Support Certain relatives outside the 'family' (as defined above) are **'liable to maintain'** an Income Support claimant. This enables the DSS to recover money it has paid out in Income Support from the liable relative, although it may in practice try to ensure that the liable relative pays maintenance directly to the claimant.

These provisions do not affect entitlement directly although they can affect the level of benefit if the liable relative does pay maintenance to the claimant. In fact, if the maintenance is high enough, it could rule out the claimant's entitlement altogether.

'Liability to maintain' applies to:

- certain sponsors of immigrants;

- married couples: they are liable to maintain each other, although as the liability only arises when a claim for Income support is made and couples who are living together cannot claim independently (see below), this effectively means married couples who are separated but not yet divorced;

- each parent of a dependent child regardless of whether they are separated, divorced or were ever married.

These rules and their application were tightened up during 1990. The White paper 'Children Come First' proposes further changes to the way that maintenance is enforced but the basic principles outlined above still stand. Recent changes are briefly discussed in the main text of this paper and in a separate FPSC Briefing Paper on the Child Support Bill, which at the time of writing, is making its way through Parliament.

The Claim
Only an individual who fulfils the rules of entitlement can be the claimant but this does not mean any such individual. Only one of the partners in a couple (see 'family' above) can be the claimant, even if they would each have fulfilled the conditions of entitlement. If they both qualify, they can choose who claims.

Entitlement
Apart from the means-test, entitlement is based on being out of full-time employment; and, subject to certain important exceptions, on being available for, and actively seeking, employment. The means-test rules apply in a variety of ways to the claimant and to the 'family', eg, the capital limit for a couple is the same as for a single person but the income test varies according to 'family' size and type (see Coverage). If either member of a couple is in full-time paid work, neither is entitled but the 'available for employment'etc. condition only applies to the claimant. Lone parents and ICA claimants are among those who are exempt from the 'available for work' etc. condition.

Coverage

The individual claimant and any 'family' are covered by the benefit payment. The rate for a couple is about 60% higher than the rate for a single person aged over 25. Single, childless claimants under 25 receive a lower rate of benefit which is roughly half the couple rate. 16-17 year olds cannot claim unless they fall into one of the categories specified by the rules and then receive, at most, the lower rate. The rates for children vary according to their age.

Premiums   *There is also an extra weekly addition for families with children, known as a 'Family Premium' and an additional Premium for lone parents, which do not vary with the number of children. There are various other Premiums, including one for carers, which chiefly means those receiving ICA, or who would be but for the fact that they are receiving another earnings-replacement benefit. There is also a Severe Disability Premium which is paid at the same rate as ICA and is not payable if someone else is getting ICA on the disabled person's account. It is also not payable if the disabled person lives as a 'non-dependant' in someone else's household (see Housing Benefit).*

Payment

The claimant receives the payment.

Housing Benefit   Help with housing costs is mostly provided through Housing Benefit (although some, such as mortgage interest, are only covered by Income Support). There are no 'liable relative' rules in Housing Benefit but the 'non-dependant' rules recognise people outside the 'family' as defined above.

A **'non-dependant'** is a person who lives with the claimant, is not part of the 'family' as defined above but is treated as closely connected or 'quasi-family'. This basically means someone who lives in the claimant's household on a non-commercial basis whether they are related or not. It could, for example, include adult sons and daughters who have not yet left the parental home.

A non-dependant cannot receive Housing Benefit in his/

her own right because s/he is not regarded as legally liable for the rent. At the same time, a claimant's Housing Benefit is reduced if there is a non-dependant in the household, on the assumption that the 'non-dependant' is contributing towards the rent. The reduction is made regardless of whether such a contribution is made, although if the non-dependant is in a low-paid job or on benefit, the deduction is made at a lower rate. In certain other circumstances,eg, if the non-dependant receives the under 25 rate of Income Support, no deduction is made.

Joint tenants who share responsibility for the rent to the landlord are *not* non-dependants and can claim Housing Benefit on their share of the rent. Those who pay rent to the claimant on a commercial basis, such as sub-tenants, are not non-dependants either and their rent is treated as the claimant's income.

The Claim
See Income Support.

Entitlement
Apart from the means-test, entitlement is based on being liable for the rent, which includes the partner of someone who is liable. Recipients of Income Support usually have their rent paid in full (unless there are non-dependants or the level of the rent is regarded as 'unreasonable'). The means-test which applies to others is similar to the one used for Income Support, although there are differences eg the Housing Benefit capital limit is higher and the Housing Benefit lone parent Premium is higher; and benefit is reduced as income rises until it tapers off altogether.

Coverage
Extra Housing Benefit is payable according to 'family' size and type according to rules which are very similar to those used for Income Support except that the Housing Benefit lone parent Premium is higher.

Payment
Housing Benefit takes the form of a rent rebate when the claimant is a council tenant so that the claimant does not actually receive a payment. Otherwise the payment is

either made to the claimant or — in certain circumstances — directly to the landlord.

Community Charge Benefit The Personal Community Charge (which is due to disappear in 1994) is payable by everyone aged 18 or over unless they fall into one of the exempt groups. The level of the charge is set by each local authority but, within each authority, it has to be the same flat rate regardless of personal circumstance. Each member of a couple is liable for their own separate Personal Community Charge and, in the event of their partner not paying, also liable for the partner's Charge. A student pays a reduced Charge and is therefore not entitled to Community Charge Benefit.

The means-test rules for Community Charge Benefit are similar to those of Income Support and Housing Benefit but there are no 'liable relative' rules and no 'non-dependant' deductions.

The Claim
As Income Support and Housing Benefit, that is, in a couple, only one can be the claimant.

Entitlement
Apart from the means-test, entitlement is based on liability to pay the Charge. In couples, this means the partners' combined charge. The means-test rules, as for the other two benefits, are based on the claimant and his/her 'family'. This is the case even if only one partner is liable to pay the charge.

Coverage
The level of payment depends on the type and size of 'family', according to rules which are similar to those used for Housing Benefit.

Payment
Payment differs from Income Support and Housing Benefit in that, in a couple, it is split and paid to each in proportion to the charge that they are each due to pay.

Family Credit   **The Claim**
Only lone parents and couples with a dependent child
(see 'family' above) can claim. Couples have to make a
joint claim in the sense that they must both sign the claim
form although DSS practice is to refer to the woman as
the claimant because she normally receives the payment.

Entitlement
Apart from the means test, entitlement is based on being
a parent in full-time employment. In a couple, at least
one partner has to be in full-time employment. The
means-test rules are similar to those used for Income
Support. There are no Premiums, however, but lone
parents are more generously treated than for Income
Support purposes; they are, for example, entitled to as
much income as a couple before benefit starts to be
reduced.

Coverage
The level of payment varies according to the size and
type of 'family', according to rules which are similar to
those used for Income Support. A major difference is
that lone parents are more generously treated (see
Entitlement above).

Payment
Payment is made to the individual if the claimant is a
lone parent. In the case of a couple, it is normally made
to the mother but the father's name is shown as
alternative payee unless the mother states in writing that
she would like his name removed.

**3
Categorical
Benefits**
There are a number of categorical benefits which are not
described here. ICA and SDA, which are described
below, are the only two which are normally categorised
as earnings-replacement benefits and the N.I. rules
about not receiving two at the same time therefore also
apply to these two benefits.

Child Benefit
The definition of a **dependent child** for Child Benefit
purposes pervades the social security system. Basically,
a dependent child is anyone under age 16 or aged 16-18
in full-time, secondary education. The child does not

have to be related to the claimant; the main requirement is simply that the claimant is responsible for the child.

The additions for children paid with some National Insurance and some Categorical benefits are directly tied to the receipt of Child Benefit and the main difference in the case of the means-tested benefits is that a claimant cannot be treated as responsible for a child who does not live with him/her.

The Claim
Any individual who fulfils the conditions of entitlement in relation to the child can put in a claim. It is possible that several people could qualify and therefore put in a claim in for the same child. But as only one person can be entitled to the benefit (i.e. it cannot be split), there is a system of priorities for deciding who. In couples who live together, for example, it is the mother. Claimants take priority in the following order:

a person who lives with the child;

a wife, where she lives with the husband;

a parent (including step and adoptive);

a mother in a cohabiting couple;

a person agreed by those entitled;

a person selected by the DSS.

Entitlement
Entitlement is based on being responsible for a child, that is, either the child lives with the claimant or s/he contributes towards the child's maintenance at a weekly rate at least equal to the rate of benefit.

Coverage
From April 1991, Child Benefit is to be paid at a single flat rate for all children; the payment for the first child is higher than for others. One Parent Benefit, which is a separate benefit but is usually paid with Child Benefit is available to lone parents (defined as for means-tested benefits) at a rate which does not vary with family size.

Payment
Child Benefit is paid to the claimant. In couples who live together this is normally the mother and, when it is, the father's name is shown as alternative payee unless the mother specifies in writing that she would like his name removed.

Invalid Care Allowance (ICA)

The Claim
Any individual carer — regardless of other relationships — who fulfils the rules of entitlement can be the claimant.

Entitlement
Entitlement is based on caring at least 35 hours a week for a severely disabled person who need not be related to, nor live in the same household as the claimant but must receive Attendance Allowance.

[AA is a benefit for a person who requires frequent attention throughout the day in connection with bodily functions or continued supervision in order to avoid substantial danger to themselves and others. Entitlement is therefore based on the need for care but the disabled person does not have to have a carer in order to qualify and need not spend the money on care. It is to be merged with Mobility Allowance into a new benefit called Disability Living Allowance.]

Coverage
As Invalidity Benefit (see under National Insurance benefits above) except that the rules relating to a child carer are slightly different.

Payment
The claimant receives the payment and any addition.

Severe Disablement Allowance

The Claim
Any individual — regardless of relationships — who fulfils the conditions of entitlement can be the claimant.

Entitlement
Entitlement is based on being severely disabled and unable to fulfil the contribution conditions for other

disability benefits. [Rates of payment vary according to age, with those under age 40 being entitled to the highest rates.]

Coverage
As Invalidity Benefit.

Payment
The claimant receives the payment and any addition.

**4
Employer-
Administered
Benefits**

Statutory Sick Pay and Statutory Maternity Pay, which have largely replaced the National Insurance Sickness Benefit and Maternity Allowance, are entirely based on the individual. Entitlement is based on the individual's record of employment with a particular employer instead of on his/her contribution record and no additions are payable.

Note on Making the Claim and Receiving the Payment

Although a partner for whom an addition or higher payment is made does not normally receive any payment, the Department of Social Security (DSS) does have power to direct that the payment, or part of it, can be paid to the partner (or someone else), if it considers it necessary for protecting the interests of the claimant or anyone covered by the benefit.

In practice this is a power which the Department would only be likely to use in extreme circumstances, for example, if the claimant was alcoholic and there were children involved. It is in any case an option open to the DSS and not a right of the partner.

In practice, the person who receives or has access to the payment may be different from the ones listed above for a number of other reasons. The method of payment is one. For example, if payment is made into a joint bank account, the person in a couple who in practice has access most readily to the money may not be the same as if the payment is made by means of an order book which is cashed at the Post Office.

Benefit is currently paid by 4 methods: order book, girocheque, automated credit transfer (ACT) to a bank account and payable order. The last is gradually being phased out in favour of ACT.

ACT to a bank account is the option favoured by the DSS as it is the least expensive and the most resistant to fraud. It is an option normally only available for benefits which have been computerised. Where it is available, take-up has been slow, however. For example, 19% of retirement pensioners, 18% of Child Benefit and 13% of Family Credit payments were made by ACT in December 1989.

Other circumstances in which a person other than the claimant would receive the payment include: a person nominated by the Court to look after the needs of another; and, where a claimant chooses to appoint someone to hold their Power of Attorney, payment would usually be made to that person.

The DSS can also appoint a third party (an Appointee) to

oversee a claimant's affairs and receive payment of benefit on their behalf. Appointee action is taken when it is evident that the claimant cannot manage their affairs (usually because of a mental disorder). The Department prefers a close relative or friend to act but others (eg a matron or warden of a nursing home, or a social worker) will be considered.

Where a claimant is capable of managing his/her own affairs but is unable to get to a post office to cash the payment, s/he may authorise a third party to act as his/her agent. This means signing the appropriate section on the girocheque or order book to authorise the agent to cash the payment. A more permanent arrangement is also available by application to the DSS.

Similar arrangements apply to making a claim except in the case of unemployment, when people are required to claim in person.

Sources   Tolley's *Social Security and State Benefits*, 1990-91;

Child Poverty Action Group (CPAG), *National Welfare Benefits Handbook*,1990-91;

Child Poverty Action Group (CPAG), *Rights Guide*, 1990-91;

All of these contain references to the original legislation and to the relevant DSS leaflets. They have been updated where necessary.

The notes on claims and payments have drawn on information supplied by the DSS.

References and notes

1   Social Insurance and Allied Services (*The Beveridge Report*), Cmd. 6404, 1942.

2   Janet Finch, *Family Obligations and Social Change*, Polity Press, 1989; Alan Deacon and Jonathan Bradshaw, *Reserved for the Poor*, Basil Blackwell and Martin Robertson, 1983; Joan Brown, *Victims or Villains*, Joseph Rowntree Foundation, 1990.

3   See 2 above.

4   Finch, see 2 above.

5   Deacon and Bradshaw, see 2 above.

6   Brown, see 2 above.

7   Information provided by the Abbey National Plc

8   Family trends have been documented in a number of Family Policy Studies Centre (FPSC) publications. See for example: Jo Roll, *Family Trends and Social Security Reform, 1985*; Kath Kiernan and Malcom Wicks, *Family Change and Future Policy*, Joseph Rowntree Foundation in association with FPSC, 1990; See also: John Ermisch, *Fewer Babies, Longer Lives*, Joseph Rowntree Foundation, 1990.

9   Linda Clarke, *Children's Changing Circumstances: Recent Trends and Future Prospects*, Centre for Population Studies, London School of Hygiene and Tropical Medicine, Research Paper 89-4, December 1989.

10 Jean Martin and Ceridwen Roberts, *Women and Employment*, OPCS/Department of Employment, HMSO, 1984.

11 Figures on the employment of women with children are reported annually in the General Household Survey, HMSO.

12 Jane Millar, The Socio-economic Situation of Single Women in Europe in Eds: Margaret O'Brien et al, *Women, Equal Opportunities and Welfare, Cross-National Research Papers*, Aston University, 1990.

13 See, for example, D.N. Ashton and M.J. Maguire, *Young Adults in the Labour Market*, Department of Employment Research Paper No.55.

14 General Household Survey, 1988, Table 2.12, HMSO, 1990.

15 Caroline Vogler, *Labour Market Change and Patterns of Financial Allocation within Households*, The Economic and Social Research Council Social Change and Economic Life Initiative, Nuffield College, Oxford, December 1989.

16 See, for example: R. Jowell, and S. Witherspoon, *British Social Attitudes, the 5th Report* (Chapter 10) Social and Community Planning Research, Gower, 1988; Ute Kowarzik and Jennie Popay, *That's Women's Work*, London Research Centre, 1989; Gallup Marriage/Partnership Survey prepared for the *Daily Telegraph*, May 1990 .

17 Jan Pahl, *Money and Marriage*, Macmillan, 1989.

18 Gallup, see 16 above.

19   T. Hogarth and W.W. Daniel, *Britain's New Industrial Gypsies*, Policy Studies Institute, 1989.

20   Jowell and Witherspoon, see 16 above.

21   *Times* letters, 6 July 1990.

22   *The Government's Expenditure Plans 1990-91 to 1992-93*, Chapter 14, Para 7, Department of Social Security, Cm 1014, HMSO, January 1990.

23   *Children Come First,* The Government's Proposals on the Maintenance of Children, Vol.I, Cm 1264, HMSO 1990

24   House of Commons *Hansard*, 17 March 1988.

25   As 24.

26   The Law Commission, *Family Law: Distribution on Intestacy* (Law Com. 187), House of Commons Paper 60, December 1989.

27   On The Children Act, see , for example, Department of Health, *An Introduction to the Children Act*, HMSO, 1989; David Hodson, *The New Partner After Divorce*, Family Law, February 1990; Andrew Bainham, *The Children Act 1989:The Standing of Non-parents*, Family Law, September 1990.

28   Felicity Kaganas and Christine Piper, *Grandparents: Conciliation or Litigation?* Family Law, December 1989; Peter McCarthy and Bob Simpson, *Grandparents and Family Conflict: Another View*, Family Law, December 1990.

29   Michael Ridge and Stephen Smith, *Local Government Finance: The 1990 Reforms*, Institute for Fiscal Studies Commentary No.22, 1990 .

30   Mary Welstead, *Mistresses In Law*, Family Law, February 1990.

31   Brenda Hoggett, Ends and Means in Ed.s: John Eekelaar and Sandford Katz, *Marriage and Cohabitation in Contemporary Societies*, Butterworth & Co., Canada, 1980.

32   *Independent*, 31 July 1990 and 15 March 1991.

33   See, for example, Hoggett, 31 above; Stephen Cretney, *Principles of Family Law*, Sweet and Maxwell, 1990.

34   Cretney, see 33 above.

35   Jacqueline Priest, *Families Outside Marriage*, Family Law/Jordan & Sons, 1990.

36   Cretney, see 33 above.

37   The Beveridge Report,see 1 above.

38   See, for example, references 14 and 16 above; also, Alison Walsh/and Ruth Lister, *Mother's Lifeline*, Child Poverty Action Group, 1985.

39   The Beveridge Report referred to Social Insurance and Social Assistance.

40   In relation to the unemployed, see, for example, John Micklewright, *Turning the Screw*, in Ed. A.B. Atkinson, Poverty and Social Security, Harvester, Wheatsheaf, 1989.

41   House of Lord Select Committee on the European Communities, Report on Equal Treatment for Men and Women in Pensions and Other Benefits, House of Lords Paper 51 of Session 1988-89, HMSO 1989.

42   Social Security Statistics, 1990, HMSO 1991. (Most of the figures in this volume relate to 1989.)

43   The Government's Expenditure Plans 1991-2 to 1993-4, Department of Social Security, Cm 1514, HMSO, February 1991.

44 As 43 above.

45 General Household Survey, 1988, HMSO, 1990.

46 House of Commons *Hansard*, 13 November 1990 col.109W.

47 Social Security Statistics, see 42 above, Table D3.02; and House of Commons *Hansard*, 6 December 1990 col 194W.

48 *Children Come First*, see 23 above.

49 *Children Come First*, see 23 above.

50 At the time of writing the proposal is contained in the Disability Living Allowance etc. Bill published in November 1990.

51 See, for example, Social Security Advisory Committee Report on Social Security Benefits (Computation of Earnings) Amendment Regulations, Cm 923, HMSO, November 1989.

52 Social Security Statistics 1990, see 42 above.

53 *Children Come First*, see 23 above.

54 It has been calculated that nearly all women, starting in 1978, will earn more in their own right than the Married Woman's Pension, Heather Joshi and Susan Owen, *How Many Pensionable Years?* Government Economic Service Working paper No 65, DHSS, 1983.

55 This history of payments for maternity expenses is largely drawn from: Joan Brown and Stephen Small, *Maternity Benefits*, Policy Studies Institute, 1985.

56 Beveridge Report, para 341, see 1 above.

57 Reform of Social Security: Programme for Action, Para 5.14, Cmnd 9691, 1985.

58 *Children Come First*, see 23 above.

59 House of Commons Social Services Select Committee, *Future Funding of Private and Voluntary Residential Care*, HC Paper 257, of 1989-90, February 1990.

60 Jo Roll, *Young People; Growing Up In the Welfare State*, Family Policy Studies Centre, 1990.

61 See, for example, Gary Craig and Caroline Glendinning, *Missing the Target*, Barnado's, 1990.

62 Social Assistance, Department of Health and Social Security, 1978 .

63 Proposal for a Council Directive Completing the Implementation of the Principle of Equal Treatment for Men and Women in Statutory and Occupational Social Security Schemes 9466/87, Comt87) 494 Final.

64 House of Lords Select Committee on the European Communities, see 41 above .

65 Social Assistance, see 62 above.

66 Government Response to the Report of the House of Lords Select Committee on the European Communities on Equal Treatment for Men and Women in Pensions and Other Benefits, Cm 1038, HMSO, 1990 .

67 National Insurance Advisory Committee Report on the Question of Dependency Provisions, Cmd 9855, HMSO 1956.

68 Department of Social Security, The Measurement of Living Standards for Households Below Average Income, Reply by the Government to the Fourth Report from the Select Committee on Social Services, Session 1987/88, Cm 523, HMSO, 1988.

69 Sir Geoffrey Howe, Speech to Age Concern Conference, 23-24 July 1990.

70   *Guardian*, 26 June 1990.

71   Social Security Statistics, 1990, HMSO 1991 (most of the figures in this volume relate to 1989); and Department of Social Security.

72   Judith Freedman et al., *Property and Marriage*, Institute for Fiscal Studies, Report Series No. 29, 1988 .

73   See, for example, Jo Roll, *Lone Parent Families in the European Community*, Family Policy Studies Centre, 1989.

74   See, for example, Finch at 2 above and references 76 and 77.

75   The following studies are quoted in Jan Pahl, *Social Security, Taxation and Financial Arrangements within Marriage*, Paper presented to the European Conference on Critical Legal Studies, 1986; H. Houghton, *Separated Wives and Supplementary Benefit*, DHSS, 1973; D. Marsden, Mothers Alone, Harmondsworth, Penguin, 1973; V. Binney et al., *Leaving Violent Men*, Women's Aid Federation, London 1981; E. Evason, *Hidden Violence: a Study of Battered Women in Northern Ireland*, Farst Press, Belfast 1982; E. Evason, *Just Me and the Kids*, Equal Opportunities Commission for Northern Ireland, 1980; J. Pahl, *Violence and Public Policy*, Routledge and Kegan Paul , 1985 ; M. Homer et al., *The Burden of Dependency* in Ed. N. Johnson, Marital Violence, Routledge and Kegan Paul, 1985.

76   See, for example, Vogler at 14 above; and Lydia Morris, *The Workings of the Household*, Polity Press, 1990.

77   See, for example, Julia Brannen and Gail Wilson, Give and Take in Families, Allen and Unwin 1987: and Melanie Henwood et al., *Inside the Family*, Family Policy Studies Centre, 1987.

78   See, for example, Ed.s, Jane Millar and Caroline Glendinning, *Women and Poverty in Britain*, Wheatsheaf, 1987.

79   See, for example, *Royal Commission on Social Policy*, New Zealand, April, 1988.

80   See, for example, Peter Whiteford, *The Costs of Sole Parenthood*, Social Policy Research Centre, University of New South Wales, Report Prepared for the Department of Social Security, Australia, January 1991.

81   Tony Lynes, *Welfare Watch*, New Society, 17 October 1986.

82   The Reform of Social Security: Programme for Action, Para 3.14, Cmnd 9691, 1981.

83   This is a topic which is now under investigation at the Family Policy Studies Centre.

84   Brian Abel Smith, *Sex Equality and Social Security* in Eds. Jane Lewis, Women's Welfare, Women's Rights, Croom Helm, 1983.

85   Lord Chancellor's Department, Occupational Penson Rights on Divorce: A Consultation Paper, 1985.

86   See, for example, Mavis Maclean, *Comment in Family Law*, January 1991.

87   See, for example, Heather Joshi and Sue Owen, *Sex Equality and the State Pension*, Fiscal Studies, February, 1990.

88   Eurostat, Labour Force Survey, annual reports.

89   See, for example, 8 above.

90   General Household Survey, 1988.

91   See, for example, Catherine Hakim, *The Social Implications of Women's Marginal Work* in Ed.s, O'Brien et al., see 12 above.

92   See, for example, Family Policy Studies Centre, *One Parent Families Fact Sheet*, 1990.

93   See, for example, Jonathan Bradshaw and Jane Millar, *Lone Parent Families in the UK*, forthcoming, quoted in Family Policy Studies Centre Bulletin, March 1991; W.W. Daniel, *Maternity Rights: The Experience Women*, Policy Studies Institute, 1980; Martin and Roberts, 9 above; A. Weale et al., *Lone Mothers, Paid Work and Social Security*, Bedford Square Press, 1984.

94   *Children Come First*, see 23 above.

95   Eithne Mclaughlin et al., *Work and Welfare Benefits*, Avebury, Gower, Aldershot, 1989.

96   McLaughlin, 95 above.

97   See, for example, McLaughlin at 107 above; S. Moylan et al., *For richer, For Poorer*, DHSS Report No 11, HMSO, 1984; A. Dilnot and M. Kell, *Male Unemployment and Women's Work* in Ed.s, A. Dilnot and I. Walker, *The Economics of Social Security*, Oxford University Press, 1989; A.B. Atkinson and J. Micklewright, *Unemployment Compensation and Labour Market Transition*, TIDI Paper 143, London School of Economics, 1990.

98   The Government's Expenditure Plans 1990-91 to 1992-93, Chapter 14, Cm 1014, HMSO, 1990.

99   Quoted by Jonathan Bradshaw, *A Defence of Social Security*, in Ed.s Bean et al., In Defence of Welfare, Tavistock, 1985.

100   Abel Smith, see 84 above.

101   These debates will be covered in a forthcoming Family Policy Studies Centre Paper on poverty.

102   See, for example, David Piachaud, *The Distribution of Income and Work*, Oxford Review of Economic Policy, Vol 3 No 3; and A.K. Sen, *Resources Values and Development*, Basil Blackwell, Oxford, 1984.

103   House of Commons *Hansard*, 30 October 1990 col.484W.

104   See, for example, Ed.s Paul Johnson et al., *Workers Versus Pensioners*, Centre for Economic Policy Research, Manchester University Press, 1989.

105   See, for example, Paul Demeny, *Relinking Fertility Behaviour and Economic Security in Old Age*, Population Development Review, Vol 13 No 1, March 1987.

106   *Income Support for the Unemployed in Australia*, Chapter 14, Issues Paper No 4, Social Security Review, Department of Social Security, Australia, Woden ACT.

107   Department of Social Security, *Low Income Statistics: Report of a Technical Review*, March 1988.

108   See, for example, Ray Pahl, *Divisions of Labour*, Basil Blackwell, 1984.

109   Sen, see 102 above.

110   See, for example, Vogler at 14 above, Pahl at 16 above, and Brannen and Wilson at 77 above.

111   Charles Murray, *The Emerging British Underclass*, with Commentaries by Frank Field, Joan C. Brown, Alan Walker and Nicholas Deakin, Insitute of Economic Affairs Health and Welfare Unit, London 1990.

112   See, for example, Roll at 60 above.

113   Janet Finch and Jennifer Masson, *Filial Obligations and Kin Support for Elderly People*, Ageing and Society 1990.

114   Finch, see 2 above.

115   See, for example, Robert Goodin, *Self Reliance Versus the Welfare State*, Journal of Social Policy, January, 1985; Hilary Land, *The Construction of Dependency* in Ed. Martin Bulmer et al., *The Goals of Social Policy*, Unwin Hyman Ltd., 1989; Ruth Lister, *Women, Economic Dependency and Citizenship*, Journal of Social Policy, October 1990.

116   See, for example, Roll, 60 above.

117   See, for example, David Piachaud, 102 above.

118   See, for example, Glendinning and Millar, 78 above.

119   Bradshaw and Millar, 93 above.

120   Issues relating to lone parents are being covered in more depth in a Family Policy Studies Centre project. See, for example, Louie Burghes, *Supporting Our Children: The Family Impact of Child Maintenance*, Family Policy Studies Centre, 1991.

121   Goodin, see 15 above.

122   See, for example, Land, 115 above.

123   See, for example, Brandon Rhys Williams ed. Hermione Parker, *Stepping Stones to Independence*, Aberdeen University Press, 1989.

124   See, for example, Sam Brittan and Steven Webb, *Beyond the Welfare State*, The David Hume Institute, Aberdeen University Press, 1990.

125   See, for example, David Piachaud, Revitalising Social Policy, Political Quarterly, April-June 1991.

126   Letter from Australian Department of Social Security, Woden, ACT.

127   Ruth Lister, *Beyond Disaggregation*, Paper Presented to Rights of Women Conference, 'Beyond Marriage', London, November, 1980 .

128   See, for example, Lister, 115 above.

129   See, for example, National Consumer Council, *Of Benefit To All*, 1984.

130   For some costings, see, for example, Peter Esam and Richard Berthoud, *Independent Benefits for Men and Women*, Policy Studies Institute, forthcoming.

Occasional Paper Series